LEV YOUR DAY

HOW TO MAXIMIZE THE 6 ESSENTIAL AREAS OF YOUR DAILY ROUTINE

BY: STEVE "S.J." SCOTT

www.HabitBooks.com

&

BY: REBECCA LIVERMORE

www.ProfessionalContentCreation.com

ISBN: 1506101747
ISBN-13: 978-1506101743

Disclaimer

Your Free Gift

As a way of saying *thanks* for your purchase, I'm offering a free report that's exclusive to my book and blog readers.

Lifelong habit development *isn't* easy for most people. The trick is to identify what you'd like to fix and create a step-by-step strategy to make that change. The key is to know *where to start.*

In *77 Good Habits to Live a Better Life*, you'll discover a variety of routines that can help you in many different areas of your life. You will learn how to make lasting changes to your work, success, learning, health and sleep habits.

This lengthy PDF (over 12,000 words) reviews each habit and provides a simple action plan. You can download this free report by going to the link below.

http://www.developgoodhabits.com/FREE

Table of Contents

SECTION 1:

INTRODUCTION

Build a Better Life with a Daily Routine

Imagine what your life would be like if, instead of chaos, overwhelm and exhaustion, your days were filled with purpose, productivity and time to enjoy the little things.

This isn't a pipe dream, and it doesn't cost a lot of money (if any). All you need to do is **develop a daily routine** that perfectly blends your personality with your career and personal obligations.

But let's face it—building an effective daily routine isn't always easy. You might be so busy that you can't imagine adding *something else* to your schedule. On top of that, it's possible that the advice you've heard up to this point simply doesn't fit with who you are.

For example, many books (including one Steve wrote) emphasize the importance of having a powerful morning routine. However, some people are night owls and simply don't work well in the morning. If that describes you, you may have been made to feel there's something wrong with you if you don't jump out of bed at 5 a.m.

You shouldn't feel restricted by the notion that great work only happens in the morning. Sure, many famous artists, thinkers, writers and composers are at their most creative early in the day, but others can work just as well, if not better, later in the day— even in the middle of the night.

According to an interactive infographic on the Podio site, creativity happens during all hours of the day. Ludwig van Beethoven worked between 6 a.m. and 2 p.m.; Richard Strauss composed music from 10 a.m. to 1 p.m.; and Pablo Picasso painted between 2 p.m. and 10 p.m. In fact, Picasso slept in until 10:30 or 11 a.m. and then goofed off for a few hours before starting to paint in the afternoon.

The idea is to create a daily routine that matches your natural energy levels and gives you the flexibility you need to meet all of your obligations.

The 80/20 of a Daily Routine

Fortunately, you don't have to do it all (at least not all of the time). Some aspects of the daily routines presented in this book will work for almost everyone, but others may not work for you—and that's okay! Give yourself permission to choose the strategies that work for you and ignore everything else.

Not everyone has the same obligations or schedule restrictions, so it would be unwise to adopt a daily routine that does not mesh well with your life. If a big chunk of your day is controlled by your boss or dedicated to your family, you'll need a different routine than someone who is self-employed and never seems to have enough time to get everything done.

Regardless of your situation and the demands on your time, with a little bit of creativity and careful planning, you *can* carve out time for the things that matter most.

The key is to be intentional with how you spend your time. One of the best ways to do this is to be mindful of the Pareto principle, which is commonly known as the 80/20 principle.

The basic premise of the 80/20 principle is that you achieve 80% of your results from 20% of your effort. This principle applies to all areas of life. Right now, only a handful of the activities you do each day or week have the biggest big impact on your life—whether you're at work, at home or enjoying a hobby.

The trick is to identify these activities and focus on them instead of worrying about time-wasting activities. The great thing about this principle is that, once you're mindful of it, you learn to focus on the 20% that yields the best results.

A great way to apply the 80/20 rule is to focus on the six major areas of your daily routine:

1. Energy (sleep and renewal activities)
2. Eating (general nutrition and meal planning)
3. Exercise (participating in a regular exercise program and moving around throughout the day)
4. Routine activities (repetitive tasks, household chores, etc.)
5. Working (at a job or in your own business)
6. Fun (hobbies, relaxation or a creative outlet)

The following book, *Level Up Your Life: How to Maximize the 6 Essential Areas of Your Daily Routine*, has a simple premise. We'll show you how to identify the 80/20 activities in six areas of your routine and explain how to get the most from each experience. We'll provide simple solutions to help you cross off every item on your to-do list without worrying about "doing it all."

Who Are We?

Rebecca is the owner of Professional Content Creation, and a freelance writer and content strategy consultant for small businesses. She is also someone who *doesn't* always love to write. She's learned that the key to making a living writing isn't sheer talent or connections (though those things help), but following this mantra: "Writers write." Without a solid daily routine that includes a good amount of writing time, this book would be nothing more than a dream.

She's married and the mom of two young adults. Over the years, she's worn many hats, such as homeschooling mom, cultural researcher in India and small business owner.

Naturally creative and disorganized, Rebecca is great at organizing things on paper—and then losing the piece of paper. Routines helped Rebecca go from dreaming about things to doing them. She's convinced that if she can develop good daily routines, anyone can.

Steve (or "S.J.") runs the blog Develop Good Habits. The goal of his site is to show how *continuous* habit development can lead to a better life. Instead of lecturing you, he provides simple strategies you can start using right away. His goal is to show how you can make lasting changes by developing one quality habit at a time.

The idea for this book came from one of his favorite quotes (by Gustave Flaubert):

"Be regular and orderly with your life, so that you may be violent and original in your work."

This quote has inspired Steve for many years. What it means to him is that the better you become at structuring your daily routine, the more flexibility you'll have to enjoy life. By carefully structuring his week, Steve has a lot of freedom to enjoy a variety of activities when he's not working.

As you can see, this book is a collaborative effort between Steve and Rebecca. We both provide bits of knowledge from our personal experiences, plus we'll introduce a number of resources that have personally helped us build successful daily routines.

Another thing you might have noticed is that, when providing anecdotes, we use the third-person tense (e.g., "Steve remembers..." or "Rebecca's friend..."). We did this intentionally to make it easier for you to follow the narrative of the book. We'll admit it's a bit clunky, but you'll find it's easier to grasp the information if you know who is telling the story.

About This Book

This book is built on the premise that, rather than restricting you or robbing you of freedom, daily routines help you to live a more fulfilling life.

If you've struggled with routines in the past, we understand. As shared above, both Steve and Rebecca have experienced that struggle themselves, and overcome it. This book provides a methodical approach to help you do the same.

We'll start by talking about the benefits of creating a daily routine and introducing some basic psychology related to the many obstacles that get in your way. Then we'll dive into the six areas of life you can streamline. Next, we'll talk about how to immediately apply this material in your life. Finally, we'll provide examples of daily routines for four different types of people.

We're excited to have you join us on this journey. In this book, you'll discover how to live a more fulfilling, successful life by building powerful daily routines.

There's no time like the present to get started, so let's go ahead and dive in!

8 Reasons to Build a Daily Routine

If you think building a daily routine seems like a lot of work, you're right. This is definitely *something else* to add to your to-do list.

That said, we feel having a daily structure gives you more freedom in every aspect of your life. Instead of filling your time with meaningless activities, you'll become more mindful of each obligation and determine if it is really worth your time.

The question is: *"Why should you create a daily routine?"*

Here are eight reasons why it's important to have one:

#1. A routine makes it easier to take action on specific habits.

Getting started with new habits is hard, but if you incorporate a small change into an existing routine, you're more likely to keep the momentum going—even when you feel like quitting. Daily routines are beneficial because they keep you consistent with a new habit when you have limited time or motivation.

For instance, a routine of reading just 15 minutes every night before bed will help you finish several books per year. It is easy to follow this routine no matter how busy or tired you are; all you have to do is add this habit to your nighttime routine and find 15 minutes of extra time. This increases the likelihood that this will become a permanent habit.

#2. A routine makes you more productive.

Want to get good at something? Do it consistently. Your skills will improve *and* so will your speed.

For example, if you're extremely out of shape and it currently takes you 25 minutes to walk a mile, start walking one mile every day. By the end of the month, it will probably only take you about 20 minutes. With consistent practice, you'll get to your destination faster.

Because daily routines help you get more done in less time, they make it possible to accomplish more each day.

#3. Routines encourage creativity.

There's something magical that happens when you've trained your mind to function at certain times of the day. Schedule a creative activity for a certain time and you *will* adapt to it.

William Faulkner once said, "I only write when I am inspired. Fortunately, I am inspired at 9 o'clock every morning."

What did Faulkner mean by this quote? It's simple—when you do an activity at a certain time, it's only natural for your subconscious to connect that activity with a specific time period. Basically, you'll train your brain to function in a specific way at a specific time each day.

#4. A routine brings a sense of security.

Change is good...*sometimes*. Too much change causes unnecessary stress and anxiety. You only have so much "stress capital," so spend it on the things that truly matter, rather than on trivial day-to-day living.

People of all ages—especially children—benefit from the security of daily routines.

When you engage in the same basic routine day in and day out, the anxiety that comes from not knowing what to expect is all but eliminated.

Later on, we'll talk about a concept called *ego depletion*. For now, it's important to know that following a daily routine reduces the amount of stress that crops up when you're forced to make hundreds of decisions every single day.

#5. A routine makes it easier to focus.

When you have a series of actions you do consistently, you barely have to think about your next move. You get into the groove without even trying.

When you drive the same route to work each day, for example, the action becomes so routine it's almost as if your car drives itself to the destination with very little effort on your part.

#6. A routine keeps the pressure off.

Putting stuff off until the last minute puts you under pressure to make up for lost time.

Consider the student who seldom opens her textbook and then pulls an all-nighter studying before a big test. Not only is this bad for her health, but she probably won't truly learn the material. Chances are she'll also suffer from test anxiety.

In contrast, the student who adds the "study habit" to her daily routine will learn the material in bite-sized chunks. Her mind will have time to store the information in her long-term memory. With an established study habit, she'll go into each test confident and fully prepared.

#7. A routine makes tasks easier.

Picture this: You boot up a computer program you haven't used in a while. You fumble around trying to find the right file or program, turning what should be a simple action into a time-consuming task.

In contrast, think about a computer you use on a daily basis. You probably don't even think about *where to go*. Your mind acts on autopilot. You think of the file you want to open and you do it without a moment's hesitation.

Just think of all you've learned since you were a little kid. You perform the same basic actions—like tying your shoes—without any thought whatsoever. It's been a normal part of your routine for so long that you don't have to acclimate yourself to it—you just do it!

#8. A routine inhibits procrastination, thus reducing stress.

Have you ever procrastinated on a task because you didn't quite know where to start?

We *all* do this on occasion.

With a solid routine in place, you're less likely to procrastinate because you know what actions are required and why you need to do them.

Consistency boosts confidence. It also eliminates stress because it keeps things from piling up and becoming overwhelming.

For instance, if you're in the habit of doing the dishes every day, you avoid the stress—and overwhelm—of doing a week's worth of dishes on a single day.

As you can see from the eight reasons for building a daily routine, you can enhance every aspect of your life by taking little actions on a daily basis.

The habit of completing daily routines will serve you well in every season of life, even if your routines change periodically.

The Psychology of Daily Routines (or Why We Struggle with Habits)

If you've tried to establish daily routines and failed, don't feel bad. Both Steve and Rebecca can relate to this experience.

Your struggle is a common one—and you can overcome it if you understand the psychology behind daily routines. You see, there are many underlying reasons why you might have failed with building routines in the past. Once you understand *why* these failures occurred, you'll be able to take the first steps needed to stay consistent with your daily action plan.

In this section, we'll talk about seven psychological principles and the way they impact your ability to build positive habits. When you understand how they work, you'll recognize why you make certain positive and negative choices on a daily basis.

Principle #1: Decision Fatigue

Researchers Danziger, Levav and Avnaim-Pesso recently analyzed factors that impacted the likelihood of Israeli prisoners being released on parole.

When it was time to decide if a prisoner should be paroled, it wasn't the crime committed, the length of the sentence or the ethnicity of the offender that determined whether the prisoner would be granted freedom. The biggest influence seemed to be the time of day the prisoner stood in front of the judge. The later in the day prisoners appeared, the less likely they were to be released on parole.

The judges weren't being malicious or intentionally treating prisoners unfairly; they were suffering from "decision fatigue." As the day wore on, each judge lost his ability to make good decisions. As a result, he went with the path of least resistance—denying parole to those who appeared before him.

As you make decisions throughout the day, you'll eventually become worn down and start to look for shortcuts. Here are some of the foolish shortcuts people take when they have decision fatigue:

- Writing an angry email instead of taking the time to respond in a way that requires more thought
- Eating a fast food meal rather than taking the time to prepare something healthy
- Making an impulsive and unnecessary purchase that blows your budget

There's another possible negative outcome of decision fatigue—doing nothing. When we're tired from a day of working hard and maintaining constant willpower, we often feel frazzled and tired. In many cases, this causes us to procrastinate on major projects we have planned for the end of the day.

Why "Fun" Decisions Are Often the Hardest to Make

In the post *"How to Be Happier and More Productive by Avoiding Decision Fatigue"* by Brian Bailey, there are great examples of how making too many decisions in a short period of time often leads to poor results.

This type of issue often occurs when couples or families wait until the end of the day to decide what to eat for dinner.

Chances are you've had some version of this conversation multiple times:

You: *"What do you want to do for dinner?"*

Your significant other: *"I don't know. What do you want?"*

After going back and forth, you finally give up and go with the path of least resistance by ordering a delicious (but very unhealthy) pizza.

You could have avoided this decision if you'd created a meal plan and shopped for the right ingredients earlier in the week.

We all think we want to have a lot of choices, but the truth is that too many choices lead to overwhelm, causing people to make bad choices or shut down and do nothing.

Routines limit the number of decisions you have to make, increasing your odds of doing the right thing.

Principle #2: Cognitive Load

According to Wikipedia, *"cognitive load refers to the total amount of mental effort being used in the working memory."*

There are three types of cognitive load:

- Intrinsic, which has to do with the amount of effort a specific topic requires
- Extraneous, which has to do with the way that information is presented to the learner
- Germane, which refers to the effort required to organize information

To put it simply, the more you have to *think about* the process of completing an activity, the less energy you'll have for future activities.

The amount of cognitive load is lower when a topic requires less effort. For instance, there is a lower cognitive load when calculating 2+2 than when performing a more complex calculation.

It's important to note that every individual has a different capacity when it comes to their ability to process information.

This difference is clear when comparing novices and experts. For example, the young child who is just learning math has to work hard to solve the previous math example—even though it's a simple task for most adults.

Here's another example:

Think of the amount of mental energy driving takes for the person who is just learning, compared to someone who has been driving for several years. The novice driver has to think about every move, from buckling a seatbelt to adjusting mirrors to turning the key in the ignition and then putting the car into drive.

In contrast, a person who has been driving for several years and drives the same route to work every day can safely drive to work without even thinking about how to get there.

Daily routines help when it comes to reducing the amount of cognitive load because, in a sense, you become an expert at the things you do day in and day out.

Principle #3: Ego Depletion

We wrote about the concept of ego depletion in our book *The Daily Entrepreneur,* and the concept is worth revisiting here because it relates to many aspects of habit development—including daily routines.

In Steve's habit-related studies, he learned about ego depletion from the book *Willpower* by Roy F. Baumeister and John Tierney. In this book, ego depletion is defined as "a person's diminished capacity to regulate their thoughts, feelings and actions."

Willpower is compared to a muscle. In the same way that your muscles become fatigued with use, your willpower also becomes fatigued, and the amount of willpower you have diminishes as you use it throughout the day. Simply put, once you've used up your supply of willpower for the day, it's very difficult to exercise discipline.

This principle is important to keep in mind as you work to establish daily routines. If you try to adjust too many things in your routine all at once, you are more likely to fail.

Our advice, as you go through this book, is to focus on just one of the six areas. Don't worry about the others until you've turned your new routine into a series of automatic actions. Only then should you move on to one of the other areas of your life. Doing it this way will dramatically increase your odds of success.

Principle #4: "What-the-Hell" Effect

Willpower is an important aspect of developing any habit, including daily routines.

Unfortunately, in spite of our best intentions, we often hit a bump, slip up and fail to do what we set out to do, or wind up doing something we swore we wouldn't. This happens to everyone. What matters is *how* you respond to this failure.

The bottom line is that you have two choices: learn from this mistake and jump right back into the routine *or* succumb to what's commonly called the "what-the-hell" effect.

For example, let's say that you've sworn off sweets, but you mess up and eat a cookie. If you eat one cookie, the "what-the-hell" effect might lead to a cookie binge. Before you know it, you've devoured a whole box of Pepperidge Farm Double Chocolate Nantucket cookies.

And since you ate the whole box of cookies, what the hell, you may as well grab a donut to go with your coffee the next day on the way to work. Of course you do all of this while telling yourself that you'll get back to your sugar-free diet next week, since you've already blown it for this week. Eventually, though, you completely give up on this habit change because you feel like you don't have the willpower to stay consistent.

Sound familiar?

We know this all too well because it's a faulty logic trap we've all experienced at some point.

Principle #5: "Monkey Mind"

Monkey mind is a Buddhist term that means *"unsettled; restless; capricious; whimsical; fanciful; inconstant; confused; indecisive; uncontrollable."*

Monkey mind is an especially big problem for those who have attention deficit hyperactivity disorder (or ADHD), but most have struggled with this problem at some point.

Monkey mind can keep you from sticking to your daily routine. It often happens when an action causes you to think of a related action. The second action leads to a third, and so on and so forth. Eventually you're doing something that has nothing to do with the first action.

For instance, let's say part of your morning routine is to journal for 10 minutes. A decision to check your email "real quick" can lead to all kinds of distractions, such as clicking on a link in an email that goes to a blog post that has links to other blog posts. And of course there are the comments on the blog that you just *have* to respond to. Suddenly that 10-minute creativity routine has turned into a 30-minute rabbit hole of unproductive tasks.

Later on in this book, we'll talk about a variety of productivity tools and habits. The reason we emphasize being disciplined with your work is that you'll avoid the trap of monkey mind. Instead of succumbing to it, you'll learn to recognize when it's happening and avoid succumbing to the lure of this thought pattern.

Principle #6: Multitasking Isn't Effective

Multitasking was once touted as *the* way to get things done. People who are (supposedly) good at it often feel a sense of pride as they declare—usually with big fat smiles on their faces—"I'm a great multitasker!"

However, we now know better. Multitasking is currently regarded as a faulty practice that causes you to get *less* done, not more.

There are a few exceptions, of course. For example, you may be able to listen to a podcast or audiobook while doing housework, walking the dog or exercising. But in most cases, being present and "all in" are important if you want to be truly focused on whatever it is you're doing.

As an example, Steve enjoys listening to podcasts on his daily walks because he follows the same routes (so there's little cognitive load). However, he turns off the podcasts when he's writing because he can't concentrate on both the words in his head and what's discussed on the show.

Remember, daily routines are much more than something you check off a list. The idea here is to improve the quality of your life and the lives of those around you. If you're simply going through the motions and multitasking the whole time, then don't expect to get good results.

Here is three-step process to help you to be present with all that you do:

Step 1: Be mindful of your current focus. For instance, your focus may be your children, a book you're reading or a project at work. Be aware of what your "one thing" is at every moment.

Step 2: Push aside anything that doesn't enhance or add to that one thing. If you're focused on your children, turn off your cell phone and shut down your computer unless you absolutely need to have them on.

Step 3: Set a time limit for your current focus. Setting a time limit for the thing you're focused on can make staying focused more doable, and can also help to bring about balance.

If you're focused on your kids, for example, let everyone know you will be away from your phone for the next hour or two. Then check for messages at the end of the session.

You'll get a lot more done if you are completely present with whatever you're doing—and you can even improve your relationships with this type of approach.

Principle #7: You NEED Downtime

How regularly do you have downtime?

If your response is, *"Not very often,"* or worse yet, *"What's downtime?"* you could be in trouble.

Downtime is not an act of laziness. It is, in fact, an incredibly important factor to keep in mind when it comes to daily routines. The truth is, we need more downtime than most people think.

According to a *2013 Scientific American* article, workers in industrialized nations spend as much, if not more, time taking in information as they do completing actual work. This consistent bombardment of information makes it difficult to process things and makes it even harder to shut off our minds when it's time to rest.

U.S. employees not only deal with information overload, but are some of the worst when it comes to vacation time. Unlike the European Union, the United States has no federal laws mandating vacation time, sick leave, paid holidays or other paid time off.

The crazy thing is, even though Americans get less paid time off than most industrialized countries, it's not unusual for Americans to have a lot of unused vacation time at the end of the year. Even worse, when people go on vacation, they often feel the need to check email and, in some cases, show up at virtual meetings.

Even if you don't have an unreasonable boss, it's easy to feel intimidated by co-workers who stay at the office late and then work all kinds of crazy hours after they go home for the evening. After all, no one wants to be the last person to show up at the office each day and the first one to go home, lest they be considered a slacker.

Why are we mentioning this? Because it's important to avoid getting so caught up in daily routines that you don't have any time to recharge. Although it's true that a set schedule will make you more productive, the idea *isn't* to work like a machine and never take time off.

This quote from the *Scientific American* article referenced above provides some good food for thought regarding the necessity of downtime:

"Downtime replenishes the brain's stores of attention and motivation, encourages productivity and creativity, and is essential to both achieve our highest levels of performance and simply form stable memories in everyday life. A wandering mind unsticks us in time so that we can learn from the past and plan for the future. Moments of respite may even be necessary to keep one's moral compass in working order and maintain a sense of self."

The bottom line is that sometimes you need to do less in order to ultimately do more.

As you think about the daily routines you want to implement, be sure to leave yourself enough margin for downtime. Or better yet, make downtime part of your daily routines. With that in mind, let's talk about the six main areas of your life and how you can maximize each.

Introduction to the Six Areas of Your Daily Routine

The perfect daily routine shouldn't focus on productivity. Instead, the goal is to carefully review each area of your life and determine how to achieve maximum results with the least amount of effort. To use the example from the introduction, you want to determine the 80/20 activities for your life and spend the majority of your time on these activities.

Sure, it's important to be productive at work, but that's only one piece of the puzzle. To truly "level up" your life, you need to streamline *all* of your daily tasks and obligations. The payoff is that you get to spend as much time as possible doing what you love.

As you've probably been told, we all have the same 24 hours in a day. When you save time in one area, you free up time in another area. If you save 30 minutes on routine activities every day, for example, you'll have 30 extra minutes per day to spend doing more meaningful activities.

Throughout this book, we'll detail a number of strategies to help you maximize six areas of your life:

1. Energy
2. Eating
3. Exercise
4. Routine activities
5. Working
6. Fun

The important thing to remember is that each area is an important part of your life. When you achieve peak results in one area, it'll have a positive spillover effect on the other five.

We put them in a specific order—based on how each impacts the rest of your life—but we recommend focusing on the area that *you* feel needs the most improvement.

To start, let's talk about the one activity we spend one-third of our time doing on a daily basis.

SECTION 2:

ENERGY

The Importance of Sleep and Energy Renewal

Talking about your daily sleep patterns might not seem like an exciting topic, but sleep is probably one of the most important (if not *the* most important) aspects of your daily routine. In fact, it's the linchpin that ultimately determines what you're able to accomplish during the day.

Even if you love to work, you can't do it constantly from morning until late at night—at least not for the long haul. Sure, there may be times when you have to work extreme hours to meet a deadline, but when it comes to establishing healthy daily routines, it's important to find that perfect work/life balance.

It's been estimated that you need at least 12 hours away from work or the office each day. This is the time for relaxing, recharging and focusing on energy renewal activities. It's also time to focus on getting a good night's sleep.

The problem? Many people downplay the importance of rest. Usually, sleep is seen as an inconvenience when stacked against our numerous daily obligations.

What you might *not know* is that when you get the right amount of sleep, you will have more energy and drive to do great things in the other five areas of your life.

How Circadian Rhythms Impact Your Energy Levels

A circadian rhythm is a pattern that repeats approximately every 24 hours. It is found in most living things, including plants, animals and fungi. It's an internal body clock that regulates our sleep patterns and determines how we respond to natural light.

Circadian rhythms are fairly constant, but they are sometimes affected by different seasons, rapid time zone changes and severe shifts in your sleep patterns.

To a large degree, we adapt to different schedules due to forces outside of our control. If your employer demands that you get up early, you adapt *not* because it's natural for you, but because it's required.

What's interesting is that we all have different circadian rhythms. Some people perform best early in the morning, others in the middle of the afternoon and a few late in the evening. There isn't a right answer for *when* you'll find your peak moments.

The trick is to know at what time you work best, and then do your most essential tasks at this time.

This is where daily routines come in, because they help you both identify and maximize those peak times for the six areas of your life.

Numerous books, including one of Steve's, recommend getting up early in the morning because it's a natural high point for *most* people. But regardless of what others say, it's important to find your own natural rhythms and work them to your advantage.

For example, many people recommend exercising early in the morning, but both Steve and Rebecca find it beneficial to exercise in the early evening. Exercising at other times leaves Steve feeling drained, and Rebecca finds that exercising in the morning leads to her getting very little done for the rest of the day. She believes exercise is a good reward and stress reliever after she's already completed the day's most important tasks.

The point here is ignore the conventional advice about when you should do specific activities. Steve and Rebeca exercise in the early evening because that's what works for *them*, but your optimal time might be early in the morning.

Treat your peak hours as the most valuable by using them to complete the most important tasks on your list.

How to Get a Good Night's Sleep

I f we narrowed down our advice for daily routines to just a few strategies, getting a good night's sleep would be at the top of the list.

Sleep impacts your ability to function well in every other aspect of life. Therefore, a *lack of sleep* will limit what you can achieve throughout your day.

In fact, according to an article published by the Harvard Medical School Division of Sleep Medicine, insufficient sleep can lead to obesity, heart disease and diabetes. It can also impact your immune system, which of course means you'll be more likely to get sick.

The bottom line is that if you want to be more productive, eat better and achieve your goals, then you need to focus on getting an adequate amount of sleep.

Here are a few tips for getting started:

#1: Keep a regular sleeping schedule.

One reason routines are effective is that they turn the changes you want to make into natural, automatic actions. People who routinely sleep at the same time find it much easier to get a full night's rest. Simply put, they get enough sleep because they've trained themselves to do so.

You may have to experiment a bit to find your optimal sleep cycle. This is especially true if you have a lot of freedom with your schedule (if you're self-employed, for example). If you have a job or morning responsibilities such as getting children to school, the time you get up each day is largely dictated by outside forces.

To improve your sleep routine, determine a set time to go to bed each night and a set time to get up each morning, and then do so consistently—even on weekends.

#2: Cut the caffeine.

There's nothing wrong with enjoying caffeinated drinks (like coffee or tea), but you should stop drinking them well before the end of the day. Many people find that caffeine consumed after early afternoon causes problems when it's time to go to bed. At the very least, don't drink any caffeinated beverages after dinner.

#3: Eat foods that enhance sleep.

While you should avoid caffeine and other stimulants later in the day, you can benefit from consuming food and beverages that enhance sleep.

It's long been known that people want to take a nap after eating Thanksgiving dinner because turkey contains tryptophan, an amino acid that induces sleep.

Chamomile tea and a hot cup of milk are known insomnia-fighting beverages.

Lesser-known sleep-inducing foods include bananas, potatoes, oatmeal and whole-wheat bread. For more on this, this article has 10 foods for a good night's sleep. (http://bit.ly/N2IVTY).

#4: Block out noise.

Noise is one factor that can keep you awake at night. This is particularly true if you live on a busy street or near a train station, or if you have family members or neighbors who are up and about when you're trying to sleep.

You can block out noise by using earplugs or adding white noise. Steve recommends this white noise machine (http://www.developgoodhabits.com/white-noise1).

#5: Shut off electronics at least an hour before bed.

Being on the computer, watching TV and playing video games can stimulate your mind to such a degree that it can be hard to go to sleep.

Try unplugging 60 minutes before bedtime. Spend that time completing a bedtime routine that includes things like putting on pajamas, brushing your teeth and reading.

#6: Block out light.

The full-spectrum light emitted by computers and smartphones can keep you awake at night if you're exposed to these devices late in the day.

If you can't seem to kick the habit of being on the computer at night, try installing f.lux on your machine. As the evening wears on, f.lux reduces the amount of blue and green light coming from your computer screen to help you wind down in the evening.

You can also block out light by hanging blackout curtains or using a sleep mask.

#7: Make your bed comfortable and inviting.

Invest in a good mattress, pillows and linens. Wash your linens regularly. It's easier to get to sleep if you crawl into a nicely made bed instead of one that is a rumpled mess, so make your bed every day.

Rebecca has a friend who is terrible about making her bed first thing in the morning. She actually takes time to make the bed before she goes to sleep because it's so much more comfortable to get into a bed that is already made.

#8: Think happy thoughts.

Think of positive things as you're drifting off to sleep. You can picture yourself in relaxing scenes such as walking on the beach or getting a massage. If you're spiritually inclined, spend some time praying and letting go of your concerns.

Since sleep impacts every aspect of your life, it's important to make this a top priority as you develop your daily routines.

#9: Keep a sleep log.

A sleep log can help you identify patterns between other aspects of your life and how well you sleep. For example, you may notice that when you eat certain foods or do certain activities in the evening, you sleep better (or worse).

You can keep track on a spreadsheet, use a Sleep Chart or a freeware computer program, or simply use pen and paper. If you want to go really high-tech, try a sleep-tracking watch.

As you can see, there are many ways to get a full night's sleep. Most of them involve planning out the final hours of your day. Ideally, you want to spend this time unwinding and relaxing. In fact, we recommend creating a nighttime schedule (with preset times) with certain tasks to help you get ready for sleep.

Most of us use alarm clocks to wake up in the morning, so there's nothing wrong with using a reminder to know when it's time to go to bed.

How to Create a Powerful Morning Routine

Let's start by referring back to the example of a bad way to begin a day. Take a few seconds to think about how some of those stressors could have been eliminated before the morning:

- Turning off the TV a few hours earlier and getting a full night's sleep
- Adding a "clothes preparation" habit to your evening routine
- Filling your gas tank on the way home from work
- Preparing and packing the foods you'll consume for lunch the next day

These are just a few actions you could have done the night before. If you did them all, you would start each day stress-free and relaxed. Once you get in the habit of consistently doing these actions, you could even add a 30- to 60-minute morning routine on top of them—one that focuses on inspiration and energy renewal.

There are many options for creating a morning routine.

In Steve's book *Habit Stacking*, he explains how to quickly complete a series of small tasks that create positive momentum for the rest of your day. What you add to this routine depends upon your personal preference.

For instance, you can spend a few minutes doing some of the following:

- Reading an inspirational article or blog post
- Thinking of things you are grateful for (working on happiness)
- Journaling your thoughts
- Writing down a short list of what you'll accomplish in the day
- Sending a positive, loving message to your spouse or kids
- Meditating or praying
- Organizing your possessions or decluttering your home

The idea behind habit stacking is to identify the habits that add value to your life, put them to a logical order and do them on a daily basis.

Another approach is Hal Elrod's *"Miracle Morning."*

Frankly, some people don't want to *guess at* what they need to do every morning. They'd rather follow a predetermined schedule that others have successfully implemented. That's why many folks love Hal's S.A.V.E.R.S. routine:

- Silence
- Affirmations
- Visualization
- Exercise
- Reading
- Scribing

Hal recommends spending 10 minutes on each activity. If you do them every day, you'll begin each morning feeling inspired, energized and ready to maximize the next 12 to 14 hours of your day.

You don't have to pick a specific type of routine. You could do the actions we've just described or complete habits we haven't mentioned. The important thing is to make a ritual out of them so you don't realize at lunch time that you still have breakfast on your teeth because you forgot to floss in the morning.

Whether or not you are a morning person, getting your head in the right place with a good morning routine will help you start your day off on a positive note.

Energy Renewal (or How to Feel Energized Throughout the Day)

Energy is a finite resource. Although energy can be maintained with careful planning, when you are out of energy, you are *out of energy* and there's not much you can do about it.

With the ever-increasing demands on our time, many people feel they don't have time to renew their energy. Because of time constrains, you may be tempted to resort to energy drinks and other stimulants. They may provide a temporary boost, but you're guaranteed to end up crashing later.

Instead of coping with the demands on your time in unnatural ways, you want to build habits that match the natural energy ebbs and flows of your body. In this section, we'll talk about two strategies to make this happen.

Strategy #1: Take regular breaks.

One of the best ways to renew your energy is to take regular breaks. The key here is to do this throughout the day instead of going on one long break—like most people do during lunch.

Short breaks give your mind a chance to process ideas and take a break from constant activity. As a result, you'll be more productive and efficient when you're working, making it easier to get more done and produce better work.

In the productivity section, we'll talk about the Pomodoro method. While this technique is designed to help you stay focused on a task, it also emphasizes taking frequent, short breaks. If you have trouble knowing when you should recharge, then we recommend using this time-blocking method.

Strategy #2: Try naps.

Naps are a great thing to work into your daily routine.

In this post (http://bit.ly/19idhq4), bestselling author Michael Hyatt wrote about some of the famous—and very productive—people who were known for taking naps. Leonardo da Vinci, Thomas Edison and Winston Churchill, among others, found naps to be a great way to renew their energy and ultimately get more done. Lyndon B. Johnson took a daily nap for the express purpose of breaking up his day into two shifts.

If you tend to run out of steam after lunch, a quick afternoon nap may be just what you need to get more done in the second half of your workday.

Strategy #3: Take quick steps to create more energy.

Creating energy isn't just a matter of taking breaks throughout the day. There are a number of ways you can create energy without resorting to caffeine. Some of these might seem unusual, but all of them can make you feel invigorated when your energy levels are depleted.

- Listen to an energizing song.
- Change socks during the day. It sounds weird, but sometimes just changing your footwear can help you feel fresh and revived.
- Eat more soluble fiber.
- Have a healthy, low-carb snack. Too much food will make you more tired, but a small portion of a healthy snack will give you a nice boost.
- Wash your face with lavender soap. Studies have shown that people experience a slight increase in alertness when exposed to the smell of lavender.
- Stand up, stretch and breathe. Sometimes a quick stretch when you're tired is all it takes to get a nice burst of energy.

- Dress sharply for work. How you look can impact how you feel. If you wear a really nice suit or dress that makes you look fantastic, you will get that extra burst of energy.
- Lose some weight. *No one* likes to hear this, but often a reason for lack of energy is the few extra pounds you carry around. It is easier said than done, but losing a few pounds makes a big difference when it comes to how energetic you feel.
- Reduce stress. Stress causes fatigue. Eliminate the causes of stress in your life and you will have more energy.
- Enjoy some revitalizing green tea.
- Take a walk outside and enjoy nature for a few minutes.
- Take a cold shower. According to a recent post on Lifehack, cold showers have many health benefits, and they also wake you up. This option isn't for the faint of heart, but you might want to give it a try.

Think back to the section on the psychology of daily routines. Remember how decision fatigue and ego depletion are caused by depleted energy levels and the actions we take throughout the day?

While it's impossible to always feel 100 percent energized, you can quickly "recharge" by paying attention to your energy levels and knowing how to get those much-needed boosts when you're feeling low.

4 Steps to Maximize Your Sleep and Energy Level

We've covered a lot of information on sleep and energy in this section. Our advice is to think back to the 80/20 rule and focus on the activities that will have the biggest impact on your daily routine.

To get the right amount of sleep (and feel energized throughout the day), we recommend these four steps:

Step #1: Pay attention to your circadian rhythms.

If you aren't already aware of when your energy is at its peak, then monitor your behavior for a week. We suggest you keep a journal of how you feel and when you get the most done during different times of day. Identify the moments when you feel super productive and when you feel a lack of energy. If possible, structure your important tasks around these times on a daily basis.

Step #2: Get on a regular sleep schedule.

If you consistently have problems getting high-quality sleep, start by following the tips mentioned earlier—cutting out caffeine, eating foods that enhance sleep, blocking out noise and light and shutting off electronics an hour before bed.

You might find it's hard to change these behaviors all at once, so you should start off with one or two ideas and then go from there. As an example, you could spend the next few weeks working on the "no TV after 9 p.m." habit. Once you do that consistently, move on to creating a full bedtime routine.

Step #3: Create a morning routine filled with simple habits.

Identify a handful of habits that make you feel energized. Start your day by building these activities into your routine. Keep the routine simple and *only* focus on the habits that start your day on the right foot.

Step #4: Practice energy-renewal activities.

Make a list of a few things you can do to increase your energy throughout the day. For instance, if you're a stay-at-home mom or an entrepreneur, you can take a short nap each afternoon. If you work a regular day job, you may not be able to take a nap, but you can take a brisk walk on your lunch break. The important thing is to settle on at least one energy-renewing activity to do during the day—and then turn it into a habit.

SECTION 3:

EATING

The Importance of Planning Your Meals

Stress, combined with decision fatigue, often rears its ugly head when it comes to your diet. It's not unusual to be tired when it's time to make a food-related decision, so it's natural to go for the simplest solution—which is often the least healthy option.

For example, if someone brings donuts to work, you grab one without really thinking about how bad it is for you. It's there and it's convenient, so you eat it.

If your family starts to ask what's for dinner and you have no clue, you end up piling everyone into the car to head to the nearest fast-food restaurant or, even "better," picking up the phone to order a pizza.

One great way to overcome the habit of eating food that is bad for you is to create a simple routine that makes eating well a simple and automatic process. In other words, the best way to 80/20 your diet is to plan out your meals—long before you're ready to eat them.

Steve recently read a fiction book entitled *The Rosie Project*. The main character, Don, a man with Asperger syndrome, mastered what he called the "Standardized Meal System." The system included seven nutritionally balanced, identical meals. He did this to reduce the cognitive load—the amount of mental effort expended—of preparing meals. (Refer back to the section on psychology for a refresher on cognitive load.)

This standardized meal system made it possible for him to prepare meals on autopilot so he could eat well, with minimal stress.

Now, you don't have to be obsessive like Don from *The Rosie Project*, but you can save a lot of time by standardizing your meals to a certain degree. Even if you really enjoy cooking, you can benefit by building a meal planning routine into your weekly schedule.

Meal Planning 101

In its simplest form, meal planning is simply creating a list of the meals and snacks you'll eat over the course of a week and making a shopping list of all of the ingredients needed to prepare those meals.

It's a good idea to set aside a certain day of the week for meal planning and another for shopping. Treat both activities like regular appointments and you'll be more likely to get them done.

Meal planning and shopping both take time, but they will save you a lot of time and eliminate frustration in the long run. You'll also eliminate the dread you typically feel when the clock strikes six and you have no clue what to prepare for dinner.

There are many systems for meal planning, so the main thing is to find one that works for you.

For many years, Rebecca planned to have different types of food on different nights of the week (e.g., Mexican for dinner on Monday, Italian on Tuesday, vegetarian foods on Wednesday, etc.). This made the process of coming up with menu ideas easier and provided a decent amount of variety for her family.

Another thing she has done is subscribe to some services that provide meal plans. Here are a few interesting options:

- Relish (http://www.relishrelish.com)
- Cook Smarts (http://www.cooksmarts.com)
- Saving Dinner (http://savingdinner.com)
- Hello Fresh (http://www.hellofresh.com)
- Plated (https://www.plated.com)

And finally, when both kids were still at home, she often got together with a friend to do "Once-a-Month Cooking." (http://www.once-a-monthcooking.com)

Now that she and her husband are empty nesters, they don't need the same level of intensity with meal planning, but they still find it necessary to create a list of meals and snacks. Then they make weekly trips to the grocery store.

The bottom line is that you need to plan your eating and have a daily and weekly routine in place to make the plan a reality.

The good news is that what you prepare doesn't have to be complicated, time-consuming, or expensive. You, like Don from *The Rosie Project*, can eat the same seven meals over and over again, or you can prepare brand-new meals each day. The point here is to identify the foods you want to eat and create a plan to help you spend as little time as possible cooking them.

To elaborate on the meal-planning idea, we'll cover a few suggestions for each part of the day in the next few sections. Remember, these are ideas that come from *our* personal experience. If you follow a special diet (veganism, Paleo, gluten-free, intermittent fasting, etc.), feel free to substitute the foods that work best for you.

Easy, Fast and Healthy Breakfast Ideas

A good breakfast is tied to productivity, success and achievement. Don't skip out on breakfast because you're pressed for time. You'll lose more time in productivity than you would save by not spending 10 minutes preparing a good breakfast.

Breakfast doesn't have to be a five-star gourmet meal. (Come to think of it, neither do lunch or dinner.) It's especially important for breakfast to be healthy and *fast*. Learn three to five quick recipes you can cook in five minutes or less. Then make sure you shop for the necessary ingredients every week.

Here are some breakfast ideas to get you started. Again, you might have your own feelings on what constitutes a "healthy meal," so substitute foods where you see fit.

Oats

Rebecca makes homemade granola using a variety of recipes she's collected over the years. She keeps it on hand so that it takes no time at all to prepare breakfast (put granola in a bowl and pour on milk or spoon on yogurt). She knows it's healthy since she makes it herself.

When the weather turns cold, she goes for hot oatmeal. That requires a little bit of prep, but it's a good standard breakfast since it's easy to keep oats, dried fruit, nuts and other ingredients on hand. Hot oatmeal can easily be made from scratch in less than five minutes.

You can even prepare oatmeal for the entire week ahead of time. Here are instructions for hot oatmeal prepared in advance. (http://bit.ly/1scQRQj)

If you prefer cold oatmeal (especially when the weather is warm), check out these tips from The Yummy Life for refrigerator oatmeal and oatmeal smoothies.

Breakfast Burritos

Breakfast burritos are a great choice, particularly since they can be made in bulk. Depending on what you put into them, you can even freeze them and then heat them in the microwave. This Lifehacker post has great ideas for breakfast burritos. (http://bit.ly/1Ac5mtp)

Eggs

Eggs are a great source of protein, and are inexpensive and quick and easy to make.

You can make eggs in a mug or simply scramble or fry an egg in just a minute or two. (http://bit.ly/1tmInqC)

Breakfast on the Go

While it's ideal to take the time to sit down and eat breakfast before heading out for the day, on some days it may be necessary to grab something to eat on the go.

Here are a few ideas for that:

- Homemade breakfast bars (http://bit.ly/1wBJrac)
- Green smoothies (http://bit.ly/MqMlyN)
- 34 breakfast recipes (http://bit.ly/1fJOL33)

Breakfast impacts your energy levels and ability to stay productive throughout the day. You might not think you have time to eat, but if you set aside 10 minutes for this meal, you'll get that time back throughout the day when you have more energy to tackle important tasks.

Easy, Fast and Healthy Lunch Ideas

Lunch is often less rushed than breakfast, but it can lead to unhealthy decisions if you tend to eat at work or nearby take-out restaurants. One way to streamline this activity (plus save money and trim a few pounds) is to plan out these meals like you would with breakfast. Here are a few ideas to get you started:

Idea #1: Leftovers

Put dinner leftovers into lunch-size containers for good grab-and-go lunches. Steve's fiancée does this on a daily basis. Not only does she save money in the process, but she's also never left wondering what she'll have in the middle of the day.

Idea #2: Salad in a Jar

Add all of the ingredients for a salad to a mason jar in the following order:

- Salad dressing on the bottom.
- Then layers of "hard" vegetables such as carrots, radishes, broccoli, bell peppers, etc.
- Then a layer of protein, such as diced, cooked chicken or chopped, hard-boiled eggs.
- Finally, salad greens such as spinach or lettuce on top.

When packed tightly, with the lid on tight, jar salads can easily stay fresh in the fridge for four or five days, so you can make enough on the weekend to last most of the workweek. The key is to keep the greens as far away from the dressing as possible so they don't get soggy.

Idea #3: Homemade Soups, Stews and Chili

Prepare your favorite soups, stews or chili ahead of time and freeze in serving-size containers (that are safe for microwave and oven use). Thaw out a serving and then heat it for a quick, healthy lunch. Rebecca likes to make a few different types on a weekend day, freeze them and have a variety available to use over the course of a month.

Idea #4: Wraps or Sandwiches

Sandwiches have been around for a long time and many of us grew up eating them—and for good reason. They are easy to prepare and make great additions to sack lunches.

The key is to have healthy ingredients on hand to make them. Buy a variety of vegetables and protein options such as low-sodium, nitrate-free lunch meat, eggs and natural peanut butter.

If you want to reduce the amount of carbs in your diet, wraps are a good option. There are even gluten-free options available for many types of wraps.

We often choose the "path of least resistance" when it comes to lunch. It might seem easier to buy a meal near work, but you can make a wiser choice with a little bit of planning. Not only does packing a lunch limit the number of decisions you have to make, it'll also save you precious time and money.

Easy, Fast and Healthy Dinner Ideas

Dinner is a great time to slow down and connect with family and friends. You may not need to be as rushed for dinner, but it still helps to plan ahead.

If you tend to be a morning person, the slow cooker is your best friend for having a hot dinner ready at the end of a hard day of work. Rebecca has used a series of popular slow cooker cookbooks called *Fix It and Forget It* with good results.

In addition to "regular" recipes, there are a variety of cookbooks in the series that cater to diabetics and other people with different dietary needs. Our suggestion is to identify what foods you want (need) to eat, then make a plan for how to make them available every single night.

As mentioned earlier in this section, Once-a-Month Cooking is another great option if you prefer not to cook at the end of the day.

If you prefer to make dinner from scratch each evening, but don't have a lot of time to devote to cooking, check out the Quick and Easy Recipes section of AllRecipes, or simple dinner recipes from Taste of Home.

As you can see, we've kept this section brief because everyone has their personal preference when it comes to dinner. What we want to stress (again) is that you should plan out your meals ahead of time and know what you'll cook—way *before* it's dinnertime.

Easy, Fast and Healthy Snack Ideas

Let's face it: We all like to snack sometimes. Some people even believe that eating several small meals per day is preferable to eating a few large meals per day. Regardless of your meal philosophy, it's a good idea to plan ahead for times when you're hit with a bad case of the munchies.

You can't go wrong with fresh fruit and vegetables. In fact, if you don't get the recommended five daily servings per day, make a point of eating them for snacks.

If you don't like eating raw veggies plain, try a dip made out of plain non-fat yogurt and some seasonings such as salt, pepper and garlic powder.

Raw nuts, yogurt and air-popped popcorn are good options as well.

When it comes to snacks, it's important to avoid buying things you know aren't good for you. Instead, keep healthy alternatives on hand so you won't be tempted when others around you are snacking on less-than-healthy foods.

As an example, Steve has a weakness for salty snacks (like Doritos), yet he never eats them because he makes sure these foods are never in his home. He knows it's impossible to eat a snack that's not immediately accessible.

5 Steps to Maximize Your Eating Habits

There are infinite options when it comes to your diet—some choices are healthy and others are not so healthy. Interestingly, the choices you make don't happen the moment you feel hungry. They're often determined by the habits you develop with regard to planning meals ahead of time.

Here are five shortcuts to help streamline the meal-planning process and ensure that what you prepare will be healthy enough for you and your family:

Step #1: Create three to five standard breakfast meals.

You don't need to be a gourmet cook or "master chef" here. Just come up with a few quick and healthy breakfast meals you can prepare in less than 10 minutes.

Learn these recipes by heart and cook them on a regular basis so you can (almost) prepare them in your sleep.

This will make it easier to incorporate breakfast into your daily routine and ensure you get your day off to a healthy start.

Step #2: Pack your lunch.

It's not very exciting, but packing your lunch each day of the week minimizes stress and helps eliminate the unhealthy decisions you often make during the workweek.

Step #3: Create a meal plan system.

This can be as simple as using a paper and pen to plan your meals and shopping list for the week. You could even subscribe to one of the meal planning services mentioned earlier in this chapter.

Step #4: Stock your pantry with non-perishable, healthy food items.

Many foods, such as canned tuna, whole-wheat pasta (assuming you're not on a gluten-free diet), canned tomatoes, canned beans, canned fruits/veggies and popcorn, are the perfect solution when you're stuck wondering what to eat. If you didn't do your normal grocery shopping, you can use any of these ingredients to make a quick meal or snack.

Step #5: Know your "back-up" meal plans.

Come up with a few "when all else fails" meal ideas to make with the non-perishable items you keep in your pantry (along with standard items you keep on hand in your freezer).

For instance, Rebecca has a quick soup she makes with canned black beans, canned tomatoes and spices. Since she always has those items on hand, when all else fails, she can make that soup in less than 20 minutes.

SECTION 4:

EXERCISE

Why Exercise Actually Matters

You might be tempted to skip over this section. We completely understand. Not everyone likes to exercise. In fact, some people despise it. That's the bad news.

The good news is that you can do exercise *your* way. What works for one person may not work for another, so don't feel pressured to follow the latest health fad. Simply focus on what you enjoy and ignore the "extreme exercise programs" often sold as a one-size-fits-all solution to society's health woes.

For instance, Rebecca's adult son is on the small side. At 5'7" tall, weighing 110 pounds dripping wet, he's obviously never been a football player. But he loves to run, and he's good at it. He's obviously built for running, while some people are better suited to other activities.

Whatever you do, don't get hung up on "how" you exercise. Instead, use this section to add exercise to your daily routine in a way that works for you.

Why Bother with Exercise?

Before we dive into some practical tips, here are some benefits to consider:

#1. Exercise can help you lose weight.

You can cut calories by watching what you eat, but if you couple portion control with regular activity, your weight loss will be more dramatic.

#2. Exercise reduces stress and other negative emotions.

If you're seriously stressed, in a bad mood or depressed, exercise is a great way to level out your emotions. According to WebMD, exercise releases endorphins, which reduce your perception of pain and help you have a more positive outlook.

#3. Exercise combats diseases and other health conditions.

Physical activity increases "good" (HDL) cholesterol levels and reduces the risk of diabetes and certain types of cancer. If you perform weight-bearing exercises, you can even increase your bone density. These are just a few of the many benefits associated with exercise.

#4.Exercise increases energy.

People often feel too tired to exercise. It might seem counterintuitive, but exercise increases the amount of oxygen and nutrients going to your brain and other tissues, leading to a boost in energy.

#5. Exercise can help you sleep better.

As mentioned above, exercise provides a solid boost of energy, so don't exercise too close to bedtime. However, exercise done earlier in the day will help you sleep better at night.

Of course, we understand that these benefits *sound* good on paper. The problem many people have is that they don't know how to incorporate the exercise habit into their daily routines. So let's talk about a few challenges that often prevent you from exercising and then discuss how to overcome them.

5 Challenges that Prevent Exercise

Steve recently polled his email list about their exercise habits. One question he asked was *"What struggles do you face when it comes to exercise?"*

The response was overwhelming—more than 400 people wrote back and described the challenges they face on a regular basis.

Honestly, there are dozens of reasons why you might not exercise. Let's cover five of the most common and suggest a few possible solutions.

Challenge #1: Not Enough Time

You barely have enough time for the important things, so exercise often seems like "something else" you have to do. Not only does it take time to do it, but you have to pack the right clothes, coordinate the activity, exert energy and shower afterward. To most people, the whole experience seems like a major hassle.

The Solution?

Start small. If you're not exercising at all, make the decision to get extra movement throughout the day. It can be something as small as taking the stairs instead of the elevator or parking far away from the building instead of parking close to the entrance.

If you do activities that don't require special clothing or cause you to sweat, you may not have to change your clothes or shower. For instance, a simple walk around the neighborhood probably won't require anything more than changing your shoes.

Challenge #2: No Support from Family

It's hard to do something alone—especially when those around you don't understand why you do it. Sadly, some people even experience ridicule from a spouse or significant other when they attempt to start exercising. It's hard to stay motivated when you feel like nobody is supporting this behavior.

The Solution?

If your family doesn't support you, get help elsewhere. In an ideal world, our families are very supportive, but if that's not the case for you, join online forums or Facebook or LinkedIn groups devoted to exercise. Attend local events listed on Meetup.com. If your budget permits, you can hire a personal trainer who will hold you accountable and keep you motivated.

Challenge #3: Extreme Weather Conditions

Where you live sometimes makes a big difference when it comes to exercising consistently. For instance, Texas in the summer can be unbearably hot. If you're a runner, it's difficult (even dangerous) to run when it's over 90 degrees Fahrenheit.

Or perhaps you live in a region that experiences extreme cold during the winter. Low temperatures and icy conditions make exercise difficult, and even lethal in some cases.

Speaking of danger, maybe you live in an unsafe neighborhood and you're concerned about your physical safety when running or walking.

The Solution?

Joining a climate-controlled gym is a great option if you are worried about the weather. Exercising at a gym is also safer than exercising in a questionable neighborhood. If finances are a concern, finding exercises to do inside your home using basic equipment or exercise DVDs may work for you.

For a few years, Steve lived in both Mississippi and South Carolina, where hot and humid weather was the norm for six months of the year. To exercise consistently, he adopted the habit of running first thing in the morning or early in the evening (with a headlamp). Neither option was "fun," but they helped him stay consistent during those spells of brutally hot weather.

Challenge #4: Physical Limitations

Not everyone is in tip-top shape. This may be especially true if you haven't exercised lately or are overweight, but it can also be true for people who have some type of injury or handicap. There are often specific *physical* reasons why you can't exercise.

The Solution?

Acknowledge your limitations and find a way to work around them. First off, you want to talk to a doctor about your issue and see what she suggests as a good form of exercise.

Next, you want to ease into this new habit. For instance, if you're extremely overweight, don't try to run a marathon. Instead, start off by walking around the block, and then gradually increase the distance you walk.

Finally, if you have injuries, find exercises that won't exacerbate them. Rebecca has had plantar fasciitis, so she has to limit the amount of running and walking she does. Instead, she attends aqua aerobic classes and rides exercise bikes at her local recreation center. Both of those give her a good workout without causing her plantar fasciitis to flare up.

Challenge #5: That Oh-So-Awkward Feeling

If you're not in very good shape, or if you're not very coordinated, joining a gym may be an uncomfortable experience. This is often truer for women, who may feel self-conscious exercising in a gym where men are present.

You may also feel unsure of yourself when it comes to things like how to use weight machines or other equipment. You might not know what to *actually do* once you step into a gym, or perhaps you feel intimidated by all the people who look like they're in peak physical shape.

The Solution?

If you're female and feel uncomfortable going to a gym where men are present, try joining a women's-only gym, such as Curves. You can also shop around for a gym. Join one with a mixed group of members who are simply there to maintain a healthy lifestyle.

If your uncomfortable feeling is based on a lack of knowledge, hire a personal trainer or enroll in a class. Many gyms have free orientations on how to use equipment, so be sure to take advantage of them.

We all have challenges that hold us back from exercising. The trick is to take time to identify *your* specific challenge and think of ways to overcome it. You'd be surprised at how often a simple shift in mindset or behavior can cause you to successfully build the exercise habit.

How to Incorporate Exercise Throughout the Day

Overall, it's important to get movement *throughout the day*—not just in a 30-minute block. The trick is to find time to do all this. What we recommend is structuring your daily routine in a way that makes it easy to get exercise during small pockets of time.

To start, buy (and wear) an activity monitor (Steve wears a FitBit). This device encourages movement by harnessing the power of accountability. When you know you're being monitored, you'll start to subconsciously look for ways to get extra movement. That trip to the coffee machine will suddenly become 100 extra steps added to your daily total. Eventually, you'll find yourself creating all sorts of reasons to get more steps.

A major reason we recommend activity monitors is because they help you build the walking habit. While many "exercise gurus" downplay the importance of walking, it's one of the easiest habits to add to a daily routine. Rather than committing to a daily 30-minute exercise program, you add a few 5- to 10-minute walking breaks throughout the day. All of these can add up to a significant amount of movement—and possibly weight loss.

As an example, Steve recently watched a CNN video where a woman lost 200 pounds simply by incorporating walking breaks into her work schedule.

Now, you don't have to take extreme measures like this woman. All you have to do is add a few new habits to your day:

Idea #1: Ditch the car.

Take the train to work and walk from the train station. Walk to your nearby shopping center. Visit friends who live within a few miles of your home. Walk the kids to school rather than driving them. Park at the *first* parking spot you see, rather than the closest.

Idea #2: Walk with friends at lunch.

Have a quick sandwich before or after a lunch break at your desk. Then use the extra time to go on a walk with your friends. You still get the socializing and camaraderie of a lunchtime break without "losing" a whole block of time.

Idea #3: Walk during commercial breaks.

Do you *really* need to see an Advil commercial for the five hundredth time? Find something constructive to do in your house during this five-minute break and walk to it.

Idea #4: Take periodic five-minute walking breaks.

Later on, we'll talk about using the Pomodoro Technique to increase productivity. One of the side benefits of using the technique is being able to use the built-in breaks to do small amounts of exercise.

The idea here is to break down a workday into a series of 25-minute blocks followed by 5-minute breaks. To make this strategy really work, get up and move around after completing each "pomodoro." Not only does this help you stay focused on tasks, it also adds a few hundred steps to your daily total. Do this 10 to 15 times a day; you'll end up walking a few thousand steps without wasting any of your precious work time.

Idea #5: Walk while talking.

With the advent of cell phones, it's easy to take conversations anywhere you go. Rather than sitting on your couch during a phone call, try walking around the neighborhood. Not only does this add steps to your daily total, it has the added benefit of adding some urgency to the call, which often keeps it focused and on-point.

Idea #6: Don't stand—pace.

If you're standing around for any reason (e.g., waiting for a bus or cab), try pacing back and forth.

Idea #7: Take the stairs.

Unless you work on the 75th floor, there should be no reason to take an elevator. Always make it a point to walk up flights of stairs whenever you're in a building. Not only will this increase your total number of steps, it'll also add some physical intensity to your day.

Idea #8: Learn while walking.

Listen to an audiobook, podcast or inspirational TED Talk during one of your walks. Perhaps you could even use this time to learn a new language. If you have a mobile phone, use the Stitcher App to stream a variety of podcasts and radio shows.

Listening to podcasts was the main reason Steve was able to build his morning routine. Instead of thinking of his walk as exercise, he viewed the time as an opportunity to learn something new.

These small activities won't take a lot of time or effort, but they do require intentionality. If you're conscious about how you manage time, you'll discover plenty of opportunities to add movement throughout the day.

Now, walking a few times each day isn't enough to get the full benefit of exercise. What you need to do is carve out time for a regular exercise routine.

A Regular Exercise Routine (Morning, Afternoon or Evening)

The *real benefits* of exercise happen when you do it four to five times a week, for at least 30 minutes each.

What exercise you choose is up to you and your physical abilities, so telling you to pick a specific program is beyond the scope of this book. We suggest that you try different activities, get as much information as possible about each one, figure out which one you like best and then incorporate the activity into your daily routine. The important thing is to create a habit with this behavior and do it on a consistent basis.

To stay on track, we do recommend a few apps and devices:

- Fitbit tracks the number of steps you take each day.
- Lift.do helps you track many healthy habits such as exercise, healthy food and drink choices and mental and spiritual practices such as gratitude.
- Jog.fm provides music to run by.
- Digifit iCardio is focused on cardiovascular health.
- Fitocracy hooks you up with a personal trainer to help you meet your fitness goals.
- Map My Fitness maps out running routes in various cities; it also includes a food log.
- MyFitnessPal is a great app for tracking both diet and exercise.
- Zombies, Run! makes a game out of running. It motivates you to run farther and faster in an attempt to escape the zombies.

Like all other habits, the best way to get started is to start small. Rather than committing yourself to a 60-minute gym routine, build the routine of *going* to the gym and only doing a few exercises. Then, when you're able to consistently do that, increase both the time required and the level of intensity.

4 Steps for Adding Exercise to Your Daily Routine

Don't worry if exercise isn't currently a part of your daily routine. You can ease into this activity by completing the following four steps:

Step #1: Add movement to your morning routine.

You don't have to complete a lengthy exercise routine first thing in the morning. Odds are, you already have a number of obligations. All that's really needed is 10 minutes of movement. You could take a walk, practice yoga or use an app like *7-Minute Workout*.

Step #2: Maximize downtime.

Review the eight ideas for getting movement, then commit to doing a few throughout the day. For instance, taking stairs, walking while talking and using an activity monitor are all simple ways to build up that exercise habit.

Step #3: Commit to an exercise plan.

Pick an activity you think you'd enjoy on a regular basis. This could be something you do at home, outside or at the gym. The key here is to pick an activity that can be scheduled into your daily routine.

Step #4: Track your success.

Use one of the apps we mentioned before to stay accountable for your new exercise habit. Don't be afraid to start small. What's more important is to stay consistent with the habit instead of trying to hit a specific milestone or exercise for a certain amount of time.

SECTION 5:

ROUTINE ACTIVITIES

Hacking Your Routine Activities?

All adults have routine activities that are necessary, but not always fun. While you can't eliminate them, you should look for the simplest, most expedient way to complete these activities on a daily basis.

"Life hacking" is a popular concept that involves looking for shortcuts and tricks to become more efficient with specific tasks. It's not just about being more productive. It can also be used to streamline those mundane tasks that often get in the way of living life to the fullest.

For instance, let's talk about organizing your home. Sure, you probably don't enjoy this activity. But if you take the time to plan out *how* to organize your home, you'll save lots of time in your daily routine.

It starts with knowing what supplies you need at all times so you won't have to make random trips to the store to buy a single item—like Scotch tape. All items will be on hand, simply because shopping for them is part of your routine.

Multiply the Scotch tape example by all of the other items you own. Imagine having every possible item you need without wasting time to look for them or making extra trips to the store. It won't take long to appreciate how much time you'll save when you're intentional about systematizing your routine activities. In this section, we'll cover a few ways to do this.

Declutter Your Home

Getting rid of unnecessary stuff (also known as "decluttering") is the simplest way to minimize your daily obligations. Think of it this way: When you have less "stuff," there will be fewer objects to clean and organize.

Now, you don't have to become a minimalist to enjoy the advantages of decluttering. You just need to get organized by putting possessions in their right places and knowing where to find everything in your home.

Reducing the number of possessions you have to fit the space available is a great starting point. It's hard to have a place for everything if you have more "things" than "places."

Here are a few ideas to get you started:

- Set a goal for the number of items you want to get rid of in a year. Rebecca's friend decided to get rid of 2014 items in 2014. She counted even little things like rubber bands—which made the task easier—but by the end of the year, her home was in good shape.
- Sort through everything you own. Get rid of items you haven't used in 30 days. Keep track of what you use in the next 30 days and then do it again.
- If you have a lot of sentimental items, keep only the best of them. Take photos of the rest to preserve the memories.

A photo album of your children's artwork or long-held knickknacks takes up a lot less space than the actual items.

- At the beginning of a new season, evaluate seasonal items such as clothing and holiday decorations. Get rid of anything broken or no longer liked or needed.

- Use electronic filing. Technology sometimes impedes our daily routines, but it also provides quite a few solutions. Electronic filing is one of them. Wireless hard drives and sites like https://evernote.com and Dropbox.com do electronically what used to take multiple filing cabinets.

- Box items that you don't use every day but still want to keep. Number the boxes and add them to a list (see the section below) so you can find them when needed.

Once you've decluttered, define a place for everything. This step is vital when developing good habits because you don't have to think about where something should go.

For instance, think of what happens when you can't find something in your home (e.g., car keys, wallet, purse, jacket, etc.) Odds are you waste *at least* five minutes each week looking for something. That's 250 minutes, or 4 hours, every year.

Steve solved this problem with his "metal clamshell habit." Now when he walks into his home, he automatically walks into his bedroom, deposits his keys/wallet into a metal clamshell and then hangs his jacket on a hook next to his dresser. While this might seem like an inconsequential habit, it saves him a few minutes a week.

Now, imagine the time savings you'd get if you had a place for every object. At first, it will be some extra work to set up this system, but you'll eventually be able to avoid those frustrating moments where you tear apart a room looking for one item.

How to Turn Routine Activities into Efficient Habits

You can save an amazing amount of time by turning routine activities into efficient habits. These don't have to be huge actions. In fact, many small habits, when done in conjunction with other habits, add up to a life that is in good working order.

The trick here is to use a concept called "habit anchoring," which is similar to what B.J. Fogg teaches in his Tiny Habits course. The best way to create automatic behavior is to attach it to a habit you've *already* successfully built.

So if you want to streamline a routine activity, you could create a statement like this one: **"After I do [established habit], I will do [new habit]."**

For instance, *"After I walk through the door, I will hang up my jacket on the second hook."*

The benefit of tiny habits is that they don't rely too much on willpower. All you have to do is pick an action that takes less than a minute and attach it to something you *already* do. When you build up a series of these small actions, you'll find it's not hard to minimize the time you spend on daily obligations.

Here are a few examples of tiny habits you could add to your routine:

"After I wash the dinner dishes, I will move the meat that needs to thaw for tomorrow night's dinner from the freezer to the refrigerator."

"After I make my grocery shopping list, I will toss uneaten leftovers and wipe down the shelves in the refrigerator."

"After the kids finish their homework, I will help them lay out the clothes they'll wear the next day."

"After tucking the kids into bed, I'll review tomorrow's calendar and make tomorrow's to-do list."

No doubt you'll want to create your own "After I / I will" statements. These directly relate to the routine activities you need to complete on a daily basis.

To get the wheels turning, here are some individual habits you may want to work into your daily routine:

- Spend five minutes picking up clutter in the living room, or any other area where stuff tends to accumulate.
- Clean off your desk. A clean desk makes it easier to get to work without distractions.
- Organize one area of the bathroom right before showering (e.g., wipe the mirrors, clean the faucets, swish the toilet bowl).
- Swiffer the kitchen and/or bathroom floor. This only takes a few minutes and keeps the floors looking decent in between more thorough cleanings.
- Lay out your clothes for the next day.
- Put your keys in the same place (remember Steve's example!).
- Pack your bags (e.g., briefcase, kids' backpacks, etc.) at night before you go to bed and put them by the front door so you don't have to hunt for them in the morning.
- Decide what you want for breakfast and prepare any ingredients the night before.
- Pack lunches and leave them in the fridge, ready to grab and go.
- Check tomorrow's weather to get an idea if you will need any special clothing or other items for rain/cold/snow. Have these items ready if inclement weather is likely.

- Keep a few small trash bags (e.g., plastic bags from the grocery store) in the glove compartment of your car to quickly gather and throw away any trash that has accumulated while you've been out and about.

- When you buy something new, get rid of something old that takes up approximately the same amount of space.

- When you use a particular food item, unless it's an item you don't normally eat, add it to your shopping list. That way your pantry will always be well stocked with all of the essentials.

- Set up a computer filing system to use everywhere. For example, organize files the same way in your Dropbox, Google Drive or OneDrive account as you do on your computer.

- Every time you shower, squeegee the shower walls before getting out. This only takes a minute and will keep your shower in tip-top shape.

- Involve the entire family in a daily organizing race. When Rebecca's kids were little, she set the timer for 15 minutes and everyone ran through the house putting things away, trying to get the house in tip-top shape before the timer went off.

- Have a designated day for running errands. Grouping errands together into a single day whenever possible saves both time and gas.

There are numerous ways to streamline habits and turn them into automatic behaviors. The Tiny Habits method works extremely well, but another great trick is to create lists for the items in your home. Let's talk about how to do that.

Why Lists

Steve thinks his dad is a little bit neurotic. He's a man who obsessively plans out every detail and has a list for pretty much any occasion. That said, you can learn a lot about streamlining your routine obligations by maintaining what Steve's dad calls his **FSD List**.

FSD is an acronym for **F**ood, **S**tuff and **D**evices. Having a list like this can add up to a lot of time savings. You don't necessarily have to use all its components, but you can improve your organizational efforts by doing some or all of the following:

#1. Manage everything with Evernote.

We consider Evernote to be the ultimate tool to manage your routine activities. It's an app and desktop program where you can add notes, images and audio recordings. Used correctly, it will help you build a virtual database of every document and list in your life.

Think back to the Scotch tape example. Let's say you maintain a list of all the supplies you use in your office. When you run out of Scotch tape, you'll update the list in Evernote. Then you won't forget to pick up this item while shopping because you've already gotten into the habit of checking your list before heading into the store.

#2. Keep a food shopping list.

This list should include ingredients for the meals you plan each week (we talked about this in Section 3). The key is to update this list whenever you cook or prepare food. This will give you a good idea of what's in your home and what you need to buy the next time you shop.

For instance, Rebecca keeps a list of pantry items, and each time she uses an item (such as canned tomatoes) she adds the item to her shopping list. This fully stocked pantry makes it easy to prepare a number of meals even if, for some reason, she was unable to grocery shop that week.

#3. Include cleaning and household supplies.

Create a separate list for cleaning and household supplies, or add them to your grocery list. Whenever you run out of shampoo, laundry detergent or another item, update your shopping list.

#4. Organize your documents.

You have two options when it comes to organizing documents: You can scan and digitize important paperwork to eliminate paper clutter, or you can maintain a file cabinet that's sorted by category. Regardless of what you pick, you should organize your documents in categories that make logical sense.

Here are some examples:

- Bills
- Check/card statements
- Tech support books/guides
- Software DVDs
- Manuals
- Maps/directions
- Reference
- Research
- Expense reports
- Calendar
- Goals
- Vision
- Project files
- Project list
- Taxes
- Legal documents
- Estate documents
- Medical records
- Contacts

#5. Label your souvenirs.

We all have objects that mean something to us. One of the tragedies of life is when you pass away and people do not understand how or why something was important to you.

A good souvenir list will not only indicate where special items are kept, but also give a brief description of why something is important. That way, once you are gone, your family will understand the significance of each item.

Our advice is to take some time to label your souvenirs. Use a label maker to add the date (use an approximate date, if necessary), location, names of the people with you and a short description of the item's significance.

#6. Keep track of miscellaneous items in storage.

One of the places a list really comes in handy is keeping track of objects in storage.

To make organizing your stored items easier, store things in boxes that are the same size to make it easy to stack them. Number the boxes and, when you list the items, make note of which box you put them in.

Rebecca experienced the benefits of this system when her family spent two months in a temporary home. When she packed up the home they left, she numbered all of the boxes and listed everything she packed according to box number. In spite of the fact that they couldn't unpack until they moved into their own home two months later, they were always able to find whatever they needed.

For example, if Rebecca wanted to read a specific book, or her kids wanted to play a certain game, she consulted her list, went down to the basement where everything was stored and went directly to the right box to retrieve the item.

You might feel that maintaining lists for everything seems obsessive, but think about all the time you'll save when you know where each item is stored. If you organize objects correctly from the outset, you'll save minutes—even hours—each week by knowing where to retrieve every item.

Why Kids and Pets Crave Schedules

Streamlining routine activities is more than organizing your possessions. It also helps you save time by putting your kids and pets on a schedule.

For example, you should have set meal times and bedtimes for your kids. If you're consistent, your children will be ready to eat when you put dinner on the table and able to fall asleep easily when it's time for bed.

This is a habit that will give them a positive benefit for the rest of their lives. For instance, let's say part of your kids' routine is to lay out the clothes they'll wear the next day before going to bed and make their beds first thing every morning. In all likelihood, they will carry those good habits with them into adulthood.

As your children grow, it will become less and less necessary to micromanage their days and lives, but there are still benefits to setting schedules for them to abide by.

Even pets can benefit from eating on a schedule. Rebecca's rat terrier, Jake, is quite the glutton. If it were up to him, he'd eat until he passed out. To keep his weight under control, she feeds him measured amounts of food at 7 a.m. and 5 p.m. While he might want (or beg for) more food, he's grown accustomed to these specific eating times.

When you organize your life, don't stop with yourself. Provide structure for your children and pets.

5 Steps to Streamline Your Routine Activities

There's a lot you could do to systematize those routine activities, so it's easy to get overwhelmed by all the possibilities and not know where to start. That's why we recommend this five-step process to streamline your daily obligations.

Step #1: Start with your biggest challenge.

Identify the routine activity that takes the most time. Whether it's cleaning, organizing or managing parental duties, you should find the part of the day that often takes *hours* to complete.

As an example, let's say you find yourself cleaning for two hours every evening after work. This should be the first routine activity you adjust.

Step #2: Streamline this process.

All routines are a series of small actions. Your goal is to break down this time-consuming routine and look for small changes that simplify it. Our advice is to use the Tiny Habits concept to create a number of small processes.

For instance, you might waste 15 minutes every night rinsing your dishes before putting them into the dishwasher. You could streamline this process by setting up a new rule (for you and your family):

"After I finish my meal, I will take my dishes to the sink, rinse them and then put them into the dishwasher."

Use this simple rule to chip away at your biggest challenge. Once you start systematizing all those small actions, you'll notice that many routine activities won't take as long as they once did.

Step #3: Track your progress.

Habits are built with consistency. Since these are smaller habits that don't require too much willpower, you can get away with building two or three at a time. We recommend focusing on not breaking the chain, and completing them on a daily basis.

There are a lot of apps to help you stay consistent, or you can track these actions on a paper calendar. The important thing is to constantly reinforce this behavior.

Step #4: Create a morning *and* night routine.

You can streamline daily activities by incorporating them into morning and evening routines. If needed, create a routine where you only do a few of these actions. Then, once you've successfully built them into automatic behaviors, add a few more.

Step #5: Add to your routines.

Jot down a list of ideas you'd like to add to your daily or weekly routines. Put a note on your calendar to review that list once a month to determine if you're ready to add anything new to your current habits.

SECTION 6:

PRODUCTIVITY

Finding the 80/20 of Your Work Productivity

In this section, we talk about how to maximize work productivity and get more done. In simple terms, the more efficient you become, the more time you'll have for the creative and fun experiences in your life.

Productivity is a topic that Steve and Rebecca covered at length in their book *The Daily Entrepreneur*. Plus, Steve provides a number of time-management strategies in his solo books *To-Do List Makeover* and *23 Anti-Procrastination Habits*. These books provide a solid foundation for maximizing your workday. So in this section, we'll focus instead on how productivity relates to getting the most from your daily routine.

Specifically, we'll talk about how to identify the 80/20 of your job (or business), and how to structure your day so those peak moments are spent on priority tasks.

What you might not know is that you start your workday with the deck stacked against you. Decision fatigue (Psychology Principle #1) and ego depletion (Psychology Principle #3) cause you to lose focus and energy throughout the day. At the end of each day, your ability to do great work has diminished greatly.

The secret to being consistently productive is to first understand how much energy each task requires and learn when you work best. Then you need to prioritize your day around completing those "high-energy tasks" during your peak moments.

It's not a difficult process, but it does involve a few steps, so let's go ahead and talk about how to streamline your productivity.

Analyze Your Energy Levels

In Section 2 we talked about circadian rhythms—an internal clock that dictates when you're at your best for different activities. This concept is important because understanding your natural energy levels is the secret to getting things done. That's why we recommend the simple exercise described in this chapter.

Spend a week keeping a log of how you feel each hour while working. This doesn't have to be anything complicated or time-consuming. Simply give each hour a score ranging from 1 to 10, with 10 being your absolute best and 1 being your absolute worst.

You should consider doing this exercise for more than a week because many factors can impact how you feel on any given day. For example, you may be in a bad mood at what is normally a peak time because of an angry email from a customer. Or you might be a night owl, but one day you randomly wake up early and feel energized. By tracking energy levels for more than a week, you'll have a better understanding of how you typically feel.

So how do you score yourself?

Here are a few questions you could ask:

- What task am I working on?
- Do I feel alert or sleepy?
- Am I happy or in a bad mood?
- Am I having a hard time concentrating?
- Do I feel focused on my current task?

- There isn't a right or wrong answer here. Instead, use these five questions to get an accurate score from 1 to 10.

After you've tracked your energy levels for at least a week, look for patterns. If you see your energy level rising over a period of a couple of hours, **that's your peak time**.

The times you consistently rated as lower are the times when you're not at your best. You can still use them to get things done, but it's better to focus on activities that require less energy and creativity. As an example, Steve usually answers email or social media comments during his off-peak times.

Finally, you might forget to log your energy every hour. A quick fix is to set an alarm on your phone. If you tend to be out and about during the day, carry an index card with you to jot things down. You can even maintain everything in a file in Evernote. What's important is to have a system and stick to it for a week.

Assign an "Energy Level Rating" to Each Task

L et's face it: Certain tasks require more energy than others. Some things can be done even when you're tired, and others are almost impossible to do when you're feeling a lack of energy. That's why you should develop a rating system for each routine work task.

The benefit of this energy level rating system is that it helps you understand what tasks to focus on during your high-energy times and which ones to reserve for non-peak times.

Take a few minutes to jot down each of your tasks, then write a brief description of each task. After that, assign each one a number from 1 (low energy required) to 10 (high energy required).

Here is a list of tasks Steve does every week, along with their corresponding energy levels:

- Writing (10)
- Editing (8)
- Podcast interviews (8)
- Mastermind meetings (7)
- Email correspondence (5)
- Social media correspondence (4)
- Tracking marketing campaigns (1)

Since Steve's peak moments are in the early morning and early afternoon, he schedules high-energy tasks (like writing and editing) for these times. Then he leaves the easier tasks (like email correspondence and tracking marketing campaigns) for the late afternoon and early evening.

There are some items you absolutely must get done in order to accomplish what matters most to you, so you should also rate each task according to its level of importance.

Whenever you start the workday, identify the tasks that have the greatest importance and require the highest level of energy, then schedule them for those peak moments. (We'll talk more about this strategy in a later chapter.)

Let Go of Outcome Attachment

In Psychology Principle #5, we talked about monkey mind— the tendency to allow distractions to keep you from focusing on important tasks.

At some point, you need to let go of the mentality that you *need* to be great at everything, or that everything on your to-do list needs to be tackled.

Part of the problem is that "experts" are passionate about many different things and, depending on whom you listen to, you'll be convinced that you *must* do x, y or z every single day. We all have projects (or tasks) we would *like* to complete, but you shouldn't feel obligated to do everything. It's better to know what is important for your job or business and focus your time on these tasks.

For instance, Steve will be the first one to tell you he has a less-than-stellar social media presence. He tries to respond to people on Facebook and Twitter, but he has found that the best use of his time is creating engaging content and talking to readers on an individual basis via email.

The point here is that you can't do everything during a workday. Striving to do so will only lead to stress and burnout. Instead, focus on what you're *paid to do* and forgive yourself if you don't have time to do everything else.

To close out this chapter, we recommend a great book entitled *Essentialism: The Disciplined Pursuit of Less* by Greg McKeown.

What this book will teach you is how to determine what's essential in your life and spend your time focused on these activities.

Use Time Blocking to Manage Your Workday

If you're a chronic multitasker, time blocking is a great way to bring more focus to your days.

Here's how it works:

Divide your day into blocks of time devoted to specific tasks. During each block, focus on one task and one task only. For instance, if your task is to clean the kitchen, don't check email "real quick" during the block of time you've designated for cleaning. You can always designate another block of time for checking email!

Both Steve and Rebecca are big fans of the Pomodoro Technique, a method of doing focused work for 25 minutes and then taking a 5-minute break. After four "pomodoros," you take a longer break (15 to 30 minutes). This is a great way to get started with time blocking.

Another option is to start with 5 to 10 minutes of work, then build up to 30 minutes of concentrated effort. The truth is, some people are simply not used to focusing on a task without interruptions. If this sounds like you, then you could apply the Tiny Habit approach we mentioned before and slowly build up the time-blocking habit.

There isn't a right answer here. What's important is to use a time-blocking method that works for you.

Next, when you get started with time blocking, you may find it difficult to know how much time to devote to particular tasks. If your task at hand requires more than 25 minutes, simply designate multiple Pomodoros to completing it. Do this enough and you'll become better at predicting how much time is needed for each task.

Finally, a great way to use time blocking is to designate a specific day (or part of the day) for specific activities.

For instance, Steve devotes his mornings to writing and every Wednesday for conversations, mastermind meetings and podcast interviews. This gives him flexibility to work on any project he wants in the afternoons of the other four days.

As you can see, there is a lot you can do with time blocking. As always, the important step is to take action. If you take the time to schedule high-energy activities and work on them immediately, the quality of your work will surpass that of people who start their days responding to the seemingly urgent tasks that don't have much value.

Prioritize Your Most Important Tasks

Time blocking works perfectly when you only have a handful of tasks. Unfortunately, we rarely have that luxury in the real world. Most of us have dozens of things to do, so it's hard to take a whole day for a single task.

Does this sound like you? If so, then you should begin each workday by prioritizing your to-do list.

To start, set aside five minutes when you arrive at your work location to make a small list of priorities. This list should include:

- Tasks that have time-sensitive deadlines (like a report that's due by the end of the day)
- Tasks that are a part of important projects (like calling a specific vendor)
- Tasks that are part of your day-to-day responsibilities (like answering emails)
- Tasks that have been previously scheduled (like sales meetings)

What goes on this list depends on the nature of your job, but it's important to think about a few considerations:

Consequences.

All tasks are simply not equal. The things that are truly important and have immediate consequences must be pushed ahead of less urgent tasks.

Difficulty.

Two tasks may be equally important, but which one should you do first? Some people like the "small win mentality" of crossing simple tasks off the list at the beginning of the day. For some, doing so provides a burst of energy or feeling of accomplishment. You can also make an argument for tackling the longer and harder tasks first. Your objective is to avoid making a decision that encourages you to procrastinate on tasks you dislike.

Energy level required.

As we mentioned earlier in the book, it's important to prioritize your tasks based on how much energy they require. Do this in conjunction with your own circadian rhythms, as explained in Section 2 (Energy).

Next, you should look at your tasks and prioritize them. In Steve's book *To-Do List Makeover*, he shares the concept of MITs (Most Important Things). Although each week is filled with a variety of tasks, he makes a list of three MITs for each day (an idea he credits to Leo Babauta of Zen Habits). Furthermore, be sure to write your MIT list on a sticky note so you're forced to keep it short!

Ideally, you should relate two of the three MITs to specific important projects, and one to an important habit. For instance, if you write—like Steve and Rebecca both do—writing is one of the daily MITs. If you're a homemaker, one of the MITs may be preparing dinner each night.

Finally, time is also an important consideration when creating your daily list. Even if you have a list of three items, one might take five hours to complete and another might take five minutes. Think carefully when making your list, and make sure you're allocating the correct amount of time.

As an example, if you have "write sales presentation" on your list, you might spend the entire morning on this task, which leaves you little time to work on the other two.

A better solution is to jot down three items that:

1. Have clear metrics (like a specific word count or number of sales calls)
2. Can be accomplished in a given amount of time
3. Are aligned with an important project

Once you've accomplished these important tasks, you can move on to the other items on your list. In the next section, we'll talk about how to do this.

When to Work on Low-Energy Tasks

Once you have a good system in place for focusing on "big-picture" tasks, you can tackle other projects that are important (for a long-term project), but not immediately urgent. Our recommendation is to keep a list of those items and work through them when you have small pockets of time.

Generally speaking, it's best to work on non-MIT tasks when you're in a low energy state. Usually this means doing them later in the day or after you've completed a particularly arduous task. (Refer back to the Psychology Principles sections where we talk about decision fatigue and ego depletion) You're not at your best, so it makes sense to do an activity that doesn't require a high level of concentration.

Here are a few suggestions for working on these low-energy tasks:

- Maintain ongoing lists for all your work projects.
- Don't rely on memory alone. If you need to do something, write it down on one of these lists.
- Arrange tasks on your list by priority. Keep the most important and immediately relevant tasks closest to the top.
- Refer to these lists before you start related tasks. This is the perfect time to make any updates.
- Sync data and lists across all devices so you have access to them at all times. Apps like Evernote, Dropbox,

Remember the Milk and Todoist are great for maintaining lists and setting reminders for specific tasks.

- Cross out or delete items from your list as you complete them. Steve does many of his lists by hand. He just loves crossing things off his list. Rebecca prefers to keep her list in digital form and check items off as completed. Use whichever approach works best for you.

- Always have a few "quick" items on your list ready to go to give you something to do when you have small pockets of spare time. One strategy David Allen presents in *Getting Things Done* is grouping lists according to context (e.g., phone calls that need to be made, tasks at home, files on the computer, etc.). When he has a few spare minutes, he rips through a list based on his context at that time.

- Rewrite your lists periodically. This gives you some time to rethink the items on your list. This is also a great "last thing" to do for the day, giving you a fresh list to work on the next day.

There are a number of ways to manage lists. While we aren't suggesting that you need to do everything in this section, we highly recommend starting each workday by identifying high-priority tasks and then allocating your energy levels effectively by working on important items when you're at a peak state.

Review Your Workday

At the end of each workday, spend about 5 to 10 minutes reviewing what you have accomplished. If you work a traditional job or are an entrepreneur with set business hours, this may be the last thing you do before turning vb b off your computer and transitioning to family and personal time. If you work from home (e.g., as a stay-at-home mom), this evaluation may take place after putting the kids to bed.

Regardless of your situation, make reviewing your day an essential part of your daily routine. During this time you can:

- Talk to colleagues about tasks related to specific projects.
- Evaluate what you have accomplished.
- Evaluate your larger to-do list.
- Do a final, quick check of email.
- Tidy up your office.
- Determine your MITs (Most Important Things) for the next day.

The end-of-day review is an activity many people skip, but it's a vital part of productivity because it acts as an instant evaluation of your time-management skills.

If you can consistently predict how much work can be completed every day, then you know you'll start to develop an intuitive understanding of what's truly important for the success of your job.

But, if you end each day with only one item crossed off your MIT list, then it's time to re-think the way you approach work. This is the time to ask yourself a few questions:

- Did I accurately predict the time required for each task?
- What distracted me from working on priority tasks?
- Are there any daily responsibilities that I can eliminate or delegate?
- If I could "re-do" this day again, how would I do it differently?

Don't be afraid to admit that your workday didn't go according to plan. Instead, use the daily review to identify the parts of the process you need to tweak. The next day offers an opportunity to make these necessary changes.

9 Strategies to Maximize Your Work Productivity

The work environment (regardless of whether you are at work or home) is filled with "noise" that can distract you from focusing on important tasks. That's why it's important to take a proactive approach and arrange your workspace in a way that helps you clear your mind enough to do your best work.

Here are nine strategies for getting started:

Strategy #1: Kill the monkey.

We've talked about the dreaded "monkey mind" throughout this book. This is a dangerous mindset where you let the thoughts in your head negatively impact the task you're currently working on.

The best way to kill monkey mind is to jot down the thought on a piece of paper (even on your to-do list), then explore the idea when you're not focused on a specific task.

Part of the reason we recommend the Pomodoro Technique is that it forces you to focus on a task and ignore all distractions. If you strictly adhere to this concept, then you don't "count" a task if you break concentration and do something else. The idea here is to teach you the discipline necessary to kill the monkey that often pops into your head.

Strategy #2: Close out email.

Email that is open all the time is too tempting. Even if you don't respond to email as it comes in, the pinging notifications are often distracting enough to weaken your resolve and break your focus. Master your email by designating specific times for it; otherwise it will master you.

For instance, Steve schedules "inbox time" for the end of each workday, long after he's completed his high-energy-level tasks. Furthermore, he has disabled all email notifications on both his email and cellphone. That way, he's only able to look at email when he's ready to take action on each message.

Strategy #3: Find the right noise levels.

Some people need absolute silence, while others need white noise to block out distracting sounds in their environment. It all depends on what works best for you.

If you like to listen to music, experiment with different styles until you find one that helps you be more productive with each type of task. Steve prefers classical and relaxing music while writing, but he needs upbeat music when he's working on mundane tasks.

Strategy #4: Manage (or avoid) meetings.

Depending on your work situation, you may not have control over the meetings you attend, but if you do, keep the following tips in mind:

- Conduct meetings standing up. You can keep a chair or two in the room in case anyone really needs to sit down, but if the majority of the people are standing, the meeting won't last long.
- Set an agenda for the meeting. Send it to attendees ahead of time so they have an opportunity to propose important items before the meeting starts. This keeps the point of the meeting clear and helps prevent you from falling down a rabbit hole of tangential topics.

- Put a time limit on each topic. People will learn to get the important things out fast and focus on work-critical conversations.

- Only invite people to the meeting if they absolutely need to be there. If you have 10 people at a meeting that takes an hour, you've used 10 man-hours, when perhaps only 3 were needed.

Most meetings are an incredible waste of time and human resources. We suggest that you either avoid meetings when you can or look for ways to streamline the entire process.

Strategy #5: Avoid multitasking.

You may feel you get more done when multitasking, but countless studies (like this one: http://stanford.io/1nL4SER) have proven that people's productivity diminishes when they engage in this activity.

In fact, multitasking reduces creativity, causes a higher ratio of mistakes and makes it harder to remember important details. We recommend that you work on one activity at a time and nothing else.

Strategy #6: Know how to deal with interruptions.

You don't always have as much control over your day as you'd like. What often happens is your workday becomes a series of interruptions, making it impossible to stay productive because you constantly have to deal with them.

Interruptions range from minor irritations (such as an unexpected phone call) to major problems (e.g., illness or the death of a family member). They also include major life changes such as getting married, giving birth or making a job change.

When these interruptions happen, it's easy to fall out of your routine. Whether you fail to complete your tasks for one day or drop your entire exercise routine, interruptions definitely make it difficult to stay on track.

We all encounter interruptions, but what separates the successful people from everyone else is knowing how to handle them when they occur.

Here are a few ways to do this:

- Accept the fact that interruptions will happen—they are a fact of life. What you can control is your response to these random events.

- Create interruption buffers. Identify how you're often interrupted (phone calls, text messages, email or people in your office) and take a proactive approach that prevents them from happening when you're engaged in an important task.

  As an example, you could wear a pair of noise-canceling headphones at work. Even if you're not listening to music, this often acts a subtle signal to co-workers that you're working on something important.

- Choose the items that always (or almost always) merit interrupting you. For instance, Rebecca has decided that when her 83-year-old mother calls, she has time to talk with her, even if she's in the middle of doing something "important."

- Give yourself a break. The important thing is to allow a certain amount of time for a break and schedule a specific time (or date) to resume your routine.

- Rediscover your motivation. It's not healthy to rely on motivation alone, because it's not always possible to stay motivated. But if you're failing at your routines, it can be helpful to remember why you added certain things to your daily routine in the first place.

- Start over. If your routine completely fails and you lose all momentum, simply have the courage to start from scratch. This can be discouraging, but it is better than never getting back to it.

We all have interruptions. The important thing is to understand that they happen and to have a plan for when they occur.

Strategy #7: Learn to say no.

People often say yes when they should say no. There are many reasons why we do this—like not wanting to disappoint someone. But saying yes to everything puts a huge strain on your time and productivity. Do this enough and it'll kill the success of your daily routine.

Just remember this: Whenever you say "yes" to a request, you say "no" to something else in your life.

Of course, there might be some people you feel you can't say no to, such as a boss. If that's the case, practice the "yes, but" method.

For example, you can say, "Yes, I'd be happy to do [requested item], but that will put me behind on [another important item]. Would you prefer that I do [requested item] first, or would it be better for me to focus on [the other important item] instead?"

Keep in mind that saying no isn't rude, and there are many ways to say no without using the word "no." For instance, you can say something like, "Thanks so much for considering me for this fantastic opportunity, but I don't have the bandwidth to do it justice right now."

That approach affirms the person and opportunity without forcing you to give in to a request that isn't right for you.

Strategy #8: Eliminate inefficiencies.

There are many tasks you simply don't need to do, and it may be possible to minimize others. For instance, a housewife may feel the need to vacuum every day, even if doing so once or twice a week is sufficient.

In other cases, a task needs to be done, but not necessarily by you. Using vacuuming as an example, the mom can perhaps delegate that task to one of her older children.

If you're a business owner, or in a management position, focus on the tasks that can only be done by you and delegate the rest to others.

Other tasks can be automated. For instance, you can set up email filters to automatically delete certain types of emails. A great resource for reducing time spent on computer-based tasks is the "If This, Then That" (IFTT) website. Use this tool to create recipes that streamline many services like Facebook, Evernote, FitBit, Twitter and Dropbox. To get started, just enter a site/device that you regularly use and IFTT will provide a number of ideas for automating these processes.

Strategy #9: Use productivity tools.

In addition to IFTT, there are a number of tools you can use to reduce the amount of time you spend in front of a computer.

Rescue Time is a time-management program that monitors what you do on a computer and provides a daily report of your productivity.

Unroll.Me is a simple tool that hunts down all your subscriptions so you can look at them in a single email, unsubscribe from unwanted lists or ignore the email and keep it "as is."

Sanebox is a third-party program that works with all email clients. Its purpose is to only allow important messages to show up in your inbox. The rest are sent to a separate folder. Then, at the end of the day (or at a time you specify), it will send you a message that contains everything in the "separate" folder.

Gmail (and other email services) has a tool for creating "canned responses" for common questions. You can use this to decrease the amount of communication you do through email.

If you don't have Gmail, then TextExpander (for Mac) or FastFox (for PC) can help you quickly craft messages that are common to your particular job.

We currently live in an amazing age with infinite options for streamlining work activities, but you might have to do a little digging to identify the tools that work best for your work style and job responsibilities.

It's been said that we spend one-third of our time working. Because of this, it's critical to systematize your day so you get the most important things done first, without succumbing to the idea that you need to complete every task on a daily basis.

Being productive isn't about getting more time so you can work more. Instead, you should strive to be productive to spend as much time as possible doing what you love and spending time with the people who truly matter.

To quote Senator Paul Tsongas, "Nobody on his deathbed ever said, 'I wish I had spent more time at the office.'"

7 Simple Steps for Being Productive

Countless books have been written about productivity, but we feel you can boil everything down into a simple 80/20 process where you accomplish the important things and happily ignore everything else. To recap what you've just learned, we recommend the following seven steps:

Step #1: Chart your energy levels.

On a scale of 1 (low energy) to 10 (high energy), determine the time of day when you're at your best. Spend a week on this exercise so you have an accurate picture of how you feel during an average workday.

Step #2: Identify the difficulty level of each task.

Repeat the same process with your routine tasks. Make a list of everything you do and assign each task a number (again, 1 = low energy, 10 = high energy).

Step #3: Prioritize your tasks.

Evaluate your daily work responsibilities and put them in order of priority. Some will go on a daily task list, while others will be done weekly, quarterly or even annually. The important thing is to know what truly matters for your job.

Step #4: Use time blocking.

Schedule time (every day) to complete the most important tasks on your list. You can assign actual times to tasks that need to be done on a daily or weekly basis and block out entire days (or a week if needed) for things such as quarterly or annual planning. This step is important because you'll build the habit of giving priority to important tasks instead of working on them "whenever you have time."

Step #5: Focus on MITs.

At the beginning of each day, select three to five MITs (Most Important Things) that need to be done that day and do those first. Only when they're completed should you work on other tasks.

Also, pay close attention to your energy levels. When you feel unproductive, switch tasks and do a task that doesn't require a lot of thought or concentration.

Step #6: Evaluate Your Workday

At the end of each day, evaluate what you've accomplished. If you completed the important tasks, then stick to the same routine. But if you struggled with your tasks, identify the leaks in your productivity and plug them. Finally, before you leave work, make tomorrow's to-do list.

Step # 7: Find your stress-free "happy place."

There are many obstacles that prevent you from having a stress-free, productive work environment. The good news is, if you're smart about how you prioritize tasks, it's not hard to stay focused.

We suggest adopting a few habits: killing monkey mind by writing down random thoughts that pop into your head, closing out email notifications, learning to say no when appropriate, minimizing the number of meetings you attend, avoiding multitasking and eliminating inefficiencies in your schedule.

As we close out this section, we want to remind you again that the purpose of productivity isn't to become a slave to your job (or business). Instead, it's to get back as much time as you can to focus on the important people and fun things in your life.

So with that in mind, let's talk about the sixth (and final) area of your daily routine.

SECTION 7:

FUN

The (Real) Reason Time Management is Important

While most productivity systems emphasize the importance of being efficient, they rarely give you a solid reason "why" you should worry about streamlining your work.

If your only goal is to be super productive so you can do *more work*, then that defeats the purpose of saving time.

For most of us, and out of necessity, a big chunk of our time is spent doing things we feel we <u>must</u> do. Many people get up and go to a job each day, not because they love it, but because it's what pays the bills. But the point of "leveling up" the other five areas of your life is to have more energy and time to do the things you truly love.

While we're not telling you to quit your job and move to a cabin in the woods (unless that's what you want to do), it *is* important to evaluate your day-to-day life and determine how you can do more of the activities that personally matter to you.

As an example, you could devote the extra time to these fun areas of your life:

- Relationships—family, spouse, children and friends
- Hobbies
- Sports (recreation)
- Creative outlets such as writing, art and photography
- Spirituality, such as volunteering or connecting with God
- Traveling
- A side business

The choice is up to you. The last thing we want to do is lecture you on what should be important in your life. Instead, we'll provide a few simple ways to help you figure out how to get the most out of your free time.

To start, we'll talk about how to completely "unplug" from your job (since that's an area where many people struggle).

How to Find That Work/Life Balance

We've already talked about the importance of separating your work life from your private life. The question is, how do you do that on a consistent basis?

Here are a few simple ways:

- **Leave work behind.** Don't check work email after hours and don't bring work files home. Obviously, this is easier said than done. The best way to make sure you do this is to set the expectation with co-workers that any project can wait until the next day. In other words, when you stop treating every email or status update like it's an emergency, it will stop being an emergency.

- **Be hard to reach.** We live in an odd time when people expect to be able to reach you by text or email at any time of the day. The personal life has been replaced by an instant gratification mentality where every question should be answered in less than an hour. A simple way to fix this is to be very selective with giving out your phone number. When you give out your number, tell people that you don't always have your cellphone on you.

  If you're required to have a cellphone for work, even though it may seem wasteful, have a separate phone for personal use. Then turn off your work phone when you leave the office.

- **Divide work space from personal space.** If you run your own business from home, make sure your work space is only used for that activity. Never intermingle your personal and work environments. Otherwise, you might slip into the habit of turning a fun activity into an excuse to do more work (like looking up cruise information and then deciding to check work email for "only five minutes").

- **Record ideas, then ignore them.** If you work at an inspiring, dynamic job, it's often hard to turn off your brain during downtime. In fact, you'll often get a great idea for your job while you're supposed to be relaxing. Instead of immediately jumping on it, we suggest you record the thought (in an app like Evernote) and then ignore it until you're back at the office.

   Finally, the best way to leave work behind is to simply enjoy what you do outside of your work life. In the next section, we'll talk about how to do this.

Have Passions, Life Goals or Bucket Lists

One of the reasons people downplay the importance of personal fulfillment is that they don't have a strong incentive to maximize every single day. In fact, many people come home from work, plop onto the couch and spend the next five hours watching mindless television. What they don't have is a clear path of how to make the most of their limited time on this earth.

We suggest taking the time to identify what matters to you. There are three ways to do this:

#1. Identify your passions.

"Find your passion" is a popular phrase gurus love to throw around. That said, there is something to be said about doing what you truly love. Sadly, though, many people aren't even aware of what they want from life. Instead, they've allowed the drudgery of a 9-to-5 existence to dull their desire to do anything of significance.

You can't figure out what you want from life with a simple exercise. It's a process that often takes weeks—even months—to complete.

One of Steve's friends (Barrie Davenport) has an interesting book on this subject called *The 52-Week Life Passion Project.* While you don't necessarily need a whole year to figure out what you want from life, you can use the multitude of exercises in this book to unlock what you truly want.

#2. Use S.M.A.R.T. goals.

We get it—"finding your passion" might be too woo-woo for you. Perhaps you're someone who likes turning life goals into measurable daily actions. If that's the case, then another option is to create a series of S.M.A.R.T. goals.

S.M.A.R.T is an acronym for:

Specific

Measurable

Attainable

Relevant

Time-bound

Now we purposely avoided the topic of S.M.A.R.T. goals until the end of this book, because most people create goals that are focused purely on work-related tasks.

While setting work-related goals is important, it pales in comparison to using them to improve the quality of your life. We suggest that you set a series of goals in seven different areas: health, relationships, business, finance, leisure, spirituality and community.

If you get stuck, ask yourself these questions:

- What are your heartfelt desires for you and your family?
- What have you always dreamed of doing?
- What activities make you feel inspired and driven?
- What thoughts give you goose bumps while imagining them?
- What things have you always wanted to own?
- What uplifts you spiritually?

The key to these questions is to take action. Don't just write down an idea and say you'll do it *someday*. As you probably know, when you say "someday," it often turns into "never." The best way to achieve a goal is to treat it like a project and turn it into a series of steps.

For instance, if you have a goal to take a two-week trip around Italy, you should break it down into a series of actions:

- Create a sample itinerary of the places you'd like to visit.
- Determine how much the trip would cost.
- Look for travel discounts and potential trip packages.
- Set up an automatic savings plan for this trip.
- Use a site (like Kayak.com) to get the cheapest available flight.
- Book the hotel rooms.
- Etc.

The point here is that we all have dreams, but not many people will take the time to figure out how to make them happen. The simplest way to do what you want is to create a goal and turn it into a step-by-step action plan.

#3. Add bucket list items to your daily plans.

You've probably heard people talk about their *bucket lists*. These are the high-level experiences and challenges they'd like do before…you know…they kick the bucket.

Sometimes the best way to spend your time isn't looking for personal passions or achieving small goals. Instead, you might want to spend your time pursing those once-in-a-lifetime opportunities.

It might sound trite, but the simplest way to identify what you want is to imagine your future self lying on your deathbed.

What are the things you'd regret not being able to do? What are the things you'd be most proud to have achieved? What relationships did you most enjoy? What experiences gave meaning to your daily existence? What lives did you improve through your actions and efforts?

The point behind this exercise is to reverse-engineer the rest of your life. The "death bed analogy" is the simplest way to know what's really important and what will ultimately be a waste of your time. The items you write down from this experience will become your bucket list.

As an example, Steve has a lengthy bucket list that includes these three items:

- Hike up Mount Kilimanjaro.
- Go on an African safari.
- Run a marathon in each of the 50 states.

He'll cross a few items off this list in 2015. In February, he's joining a group of entrepreneurs, flying to Africa, hiking up Mount Kilimanjaro and going on a two-day safari. Plus he's planning on running two more marathons, which means he has 33 states to go!

Bucket lists provide an opportunity to do amazing things in your life, but you don't have to fly to a different continent or get chased down a street by a pack of angry bulls to find meaning. Instead, you could slow down and learn to appreciate the world around you. Let's talk about that next.

4 Ways to Enjoy the Little Things

Growing up, one of Steve's favorite movies was *The Adventures of Buckaroo Banzai*. (Yes, he was a strange kid.) Within this film, there is one quote that's always stuck with him:

"Wherever you go, there you are."

Now, this line has been attributed to a variety of spiritual figures, but the original source doesn't really matter. What's important is the point behind this expression.

The truth is you don't need to complete an extreme athletic event or travel to a distant land in order to experience fulfillment. Even when you accomplish a major life goal, you still bring all the internal "stuff" with you. So if you're an unhappy, angry person in New Jersey, then you'll probably be an unhappy, angry person on top of Mount Kilimanjaro. Wherever you go, there you are.

This means, in addition to moving towards a major goal, it's equally important to enjoy your day-to-day experiences. As the great philosopher Ferris Bueller once said, "Life moves pretty fast. If you don't stop and look around once in a while, you could miss it."

(Yes, we just quoted *two* '80s movies in a single introduction.)

So to enjoy the little things, we recommend regularly doing four activities:

#1: Be still.

It's hard to get clarity when your body—and mind—never slow down. But stillness is a necessary discipline and something you should incorporate into your daily routine if you want to stop going through the motions of life.

Some people opt to practice meditation as a form of stillness, others journal and still others pray and read sacred scriptures such as the Bible.

In addition to having a set time to be still (e.g., first thing in the morning or right before bed), you can also steal a few minutes here and there to think higher-level thoughts. For instance, you can practice the habit of stillness when:

- Waiting in line
- Driving
- Eating breakfast
- Walking or jogging
- On the plane
- Doing light housework

Notice that in many of the examples above your body may be moving, but that doesn't mean you can't be still on the inside.

If you need a bit of guidance and instruction, try a guided meditation app like Headspace.

#2. Live in the now.

A lot of people spend time dreaming about the future, thinking they will be happy "when this or that happens." Planning for the future is important, but don't worry about it.

Focus on one thing at a time and act deliberately. For instance, eat slowly. Enjoy your food instead of rushing through every meal. When you're in conversation, actively listen rather than allowing your mind to wander or thinking about what you'll say in response.

One great book on this subject is *The Power of Now* by Eckhart Tolle. If you have difficulty living in the present moment, then this book can help you get the most out of those little moments.

#3. Be grateful.

As mentioned in the point above, happiness is not a goal you need to achieve someday. It's something you should have in the here and now. Those who are constantly unhappy and resentful will likely continue to be that way regardless of the good things that come their way.

To foster gratitude, spend some time every day thinking of all of the things you're grateful for. Many find it helpful to keep a gratitude journal. Here's an article that explains the importance of being grateful: (http://bit.ly/1hBuqED)

Also, giving to others who are less fortunate can help you appreciate what you do have.

For instance, Rebecca's church helps provide food and shelter for homeless people when the temperatures drop to dangerously low levels.

One day when it was below zero, she felt grumpy about leaving her warm home to transport a slow cooker full of chili to the church. In that moment, she realized how ridiculous it was to feel ungrateful, considering that the people who would eat the chili are out in the cold all the time.

Take time to examine your life. Even if you're having a bad day or going through a rough patch, there is probably a lot to be thankful for. All you need to do is set aside a few minutes each day to recognize the good things in your life.

#4: Find meaning in everything you do.

Brother Lawrence was a lay brother in a Carmelite monastery. His position—kitchen duty—was a humble one, but he found great meaning in his mundane tasks because he viewed everything he did as an act of worship. For instance, in his biography, he is quoted as saying, *"I flip my little omelet in the frying pan for the love of God..."*

This is even more striking because he despised cooking but chose to make it a spiritual experience.

If you're reading this book, chances are you don't live in a monastery and cooking an omelet isn't a spiritual experience for you. But you can learn to savor each moment and connect even mundane tasks to a higher purpose.

For instance, when washing dishes, you can experience gratitude for ample food to eat and all of the other material blessings you have. When you do laundry for your family members, you can think about how they are special to you, and give thanks that they are in your life.

3 Steps to Live a Fuller Life

Getting the most from life doesn't require a complete shift in your daily routine. In fact, you can get started with four simple steps:

Step #1: Practice disconnecting from your job. If you work at the traditional 9-to-5 job, set the expectation that you don't respond to email, text messages or phone calls when you're not in the office. If you work from home, designate space in your home as office space and, from here on out, choose to work in only that one location.

Step #2: Identify where you want to be five years from now, not just in business, but in other areas of life as well. Try one of three strategies to identify what you truly want: 1. Identify your personal passions. 2. Create S.M.A.R.T. goals. 3. Maintain a bucket list.

No matter what, schedule time to work on those goals and consider how you can incorporate small steps toward accomplishing them into your daily routines.

Step #3: Find meaning in your daily experiences. Choose a way to practice stillness, such as praying or journaling. Begin to practice this daily. For best results, start small (e.g., five minutes a day).

You could also start a gratitude journal. If journaling isn't your thing, try a different tactic for expressing gratitude. For instance, make a point of telling one person what you appreciate about them each day.

SECTION 8:

HOW TO LEVEL UP YOUR DAY

4 Ways to Maximize Your Daily Routine

Since you've made it this far, your head is likely swimming with ideas for how to use daily routines to improve your life.

But as is true with all books, just reading something doesn't help you yield fantastic results. To benefit from the strategies in this book, you need to apply what you've learned. Specifically, it's important to have a strategy for incorporating all this information into the six areas of your daily routine.

In this section, we'll provide ways to get started with the material we've covered.

#1. Focus on your 80/20.

We all live hectic, crazy, busy lives, so you may feel that you don't have time to tackle every suggestion in this book. Fortunately, we have good news—you don't have to do it all. A better solution is to focus on the 20 percent of activities that will yield 80 percent of the results for you.

The point here is to identify the one area of your life that needs the most improvement and start there. Treat each section of this book as a habit and focus on building one routine at a time.

And if you feel like there's not enough time?

Then you might have to sacrifice something else to free up time to move closer to getting the most from life.

Here are a few things you can limit—or give up all together—to free up time.

- **Sleep**. This is a tricky one. In Section 2, we talked about the importance of sleep, so we're not encouraging you to deprive yourself of a full night's rest. On other hand, some people overestimate the amount of sleep they need. Try getting up just 15 to 30 minutes earlier for a few weeks and see how you do.

- **TV**. We're not dead set against watching TV. We live in a golden age of television, and there are some really good shows out there. That being said, it's easy to spend an excessive amount of time watching your favorite shows. Be discerning here. Watch no more than 60 minutes of TV per night and you'll have more time for other things.

- **Social media**. We're not out to stop people from spending time on social media, just like we're not out to get you to stop watching TV entirely. We both spend time on social media sites. The key is to limit the amount of time you spend. Set a timer for 30 minutes and log out when the timer goes off. You can also use a tool like <u>Rescue Time</u> to regulate your daily social media activities.

- **Email**. Email can be a big time sink (and distraction) for many folks. We recommend scheduling a time (or times) each day for inbox management, and only checking email at that time.

- **Work**. You don't have to quit your job to find enlightenment. However, you might be able to arrange a more flexible schedule. Many companies are open to allowing employees to at least partially telecommute. If your boss is skeptical, ask if you can do it as a trial—and then make sure to accomplish more, not less, as a result.

- **Non-Educational Reading**. Scott and Rebecca both love to read, but often this habit can be just as bad as watching television. If reading keeps you from doing more productive things, it's time to put the book down and focus on your routines.

As is true with all areas of habit development, don't try to cut back on all of the things listed above at once. Pick one or two items to free up enough time to get you started.

#2. Use nine steps to form new habits.

In our book *The Daily Entrepreneur* we provide nine steps for forming a habit. Again, we recommend this process because much of the information in this guide requires adding positive routines into your life. Here's a recap of how to create new a habit:

(I*) Focus on one habit (or routine) at a time.

(II*) Build a habit-stacking routine (optional). Habit stacking makes it possible to focus on more than one *small habit* at a time by "stacking" them together.

To do so, identify a habit you've already established and use it to trigger the next habit. For instance, writing in your gratitude journal can be triggered by meditating. When you complete your meditation time, immediately jot down things you're grateful for in your journal.

(III*) Commit to the habit for 30 days. A lot of people say it takes 21 days to build a habit; others claim it takes 66 days. Thirty days is a happy medium because some habits take a longer or shorter period of time to establish. You may want to focus on one new routine each month.

(IV*) Anchor the new routine to an established habit. You likely have many things that you already do automatically.

With this approach, state, "After I [your anchor], I will [new routine]."

(V*) Take baby steps. You'll set yourself up for failure if you try to do too much right away. For instance, if you're currently out of shape and you want to start with an exercise routine, start with something small like walking 10 minutes per day.

(VI*) Create accountability for the new habit. If you tell other people about your commitment, you'll be more likely to do it. You can also install an accountability app on your phone to help you to face up to how well you do or don't stick with your routines.

(VII*) Overcome setbacks with an "if/then" plan. Identify obstacles that often get in your way and then make a plan for how you'll overcome them.

For example, if you find that email pulls you away from the work you need to do, your if/then plan could be, "If I'm distracted by email, I won't check it until I get [your new routine] done."

(IIX*) Reward important milestones. Reward yourself for consistently doing a routine for a set period of time. Rewards don't have to be expensive. They can be something simple like going on a movie date or buying a new novel.

(IX*) Build a new identity. Discipline will only get you so far when it comes to sticking to your daily routines. When you tie your routine to who you are as a person, you'll find it much easier to be consistent. For instance, Steve is most proud of two of his identity-based habits: running and writing. It's not always fun to do those activities day in and day out, but he does them consistently because it's who he is.

#3. Take advantage of mornings and evenings.

When it comes to daily routines, your mornings and evenings are the most important part of your day. A solid morning routine gets your day off to a good start, while a good evening routine lays the foundation for a powerful start to the next day.

Morning routines are typically made up of small tasks such as eating breakfast, showering and making your bed.

Before you move into the "work" aspect of your day, complete five minutes of journaling to gain clarity on what's important for the forthcoming day. You can use this time to:

- List the work tasks you need to accomplish today.
- Make note of any personal obligations.
- Evaluate things on your to-do list to make sure they fit with your long-term goals.

- Jot down one *fun thing* you want to do.
- At the end of the day (or the workday), evaluate how you did by answering these questions:
- Did I accurately predict the time required for each task?
- What distracted me from working on priority tasks?
- Are there any daily responsibilities that I can eliminate or delegate?
- If I could "re-do" this day again, how would I do it differently?

Writing down your thoughts might seem like an extra activity, but the benefit to doing it twice a day is that you gain clarity on where to best focus your energy.

#4. Keep track of your new routines.

It's hard to keep up with new habits and routines if you don't have them in writing.

We suggest that you write everything down and monitor these changes on a daily basis. Not only will this hold you accountable, it will also give you a strong sense of accomplishment and motivation as you introduce positive routines into your life.

Your routines can be handwritten, typed in a word processing program (like Word, Pages or Google Docs) or stored in a mobile app.

Rebecca created an OneNote template for her routines. The template lists each part of her routine and has a handy little checkbox next to each item (she loves checking things off!). Each morning, she loads the template into a fresh OneNote page and then checks things off as she completes them.

On the other hand, Steve prefers to only track the habits he's currently trying to reinforce in his life. (So he doesn't track his runs, since this is a habit he's already successfully built.) The tool he prefers is the Lift.do app.

As you can see, there are a lot of options for reinforcing a new routine. There's always the pen-and-paper or word-processing approach, but if you're willing to go high-tech, these apps can really help:

Evernote is great for general note taking, and taking notes is one of the best habits you can develop. Used correctly, Evernote can manage pretty much everything in your life.

OneNote is similar to Evernote, but it has a few different features. The reason Rebecca recommends it is that you can create reusable templates in OneNote for your daily routines.

Lift.do is a great general habit-tracking app that also has a social component to help you find partners to keep you accountable.

Chains.cc is a good basic habit tool that focuses on "not breaking the chain." It has a social component that allows you to have up to 12 people in a group. This increases accountability and makes it more fun.

Strides is another habit-tracking app. The difference is that it has robust metrics that make it easy to see how well you're doing. As you progress, you can "level up," so the app has a gamification aspect to it as well.

Throughout this book, we've tried to keep these routines as simple as possible. As we wrap things up, this advice is more relevant than ever.

Every day, you make decisions about the six major areas of your life. You might be tempted to change everything at once, but we suggest you identify the one area that needs the most improvement, focus on that area first and then repeat the same process throughout the five other areas. The idea here is to keep adding small changes that eventually build up to a lasting change in your daily routine.

SECTION 9:

HOW TO LEVEL UP YOUR DAY

Want to See Examples?

We imagine it's hard to conceptualize the idea of a daily routine. Everyone wears a variety of hats throughout the day, so you might not be sure how other people manage to fit it all in. That's why we've persuaded a few different people to talk to us about *their* daily routines.

In addition, we worked hard to get responses from a cross-section of society: a stay-at-home mom, a 9-to-5 employee, a creative artist and a self-employed entrepreneur. Each person answered four simple questions:

1. What challenges have you experienced when it comes to maintaining a daily routine for your particular situation?
2. How have you overcome these challenge?
3. Give us a sample daily/weekly routine you use you keep everything humming along.
4. In what way does your routine make your life better?

If you're not sure how it's possible to do it all in a single day, then pay close attention to how these four regular folks manage their daily routines. Some people do exactly what we recommend in this book, while others have their own idea of what it takes to build powerful daily routines. We've included each person's entire response to show what it's actually like to be intentional about how you spend your days.

(Side note: We did minor edits for grammar and spelling, but we tried our best to leave everything in the *original words* of the authors.)

#1. Stay-at-Home Mom

Name: Tanya Sites

Role: Stay-at-home mom to teens

Website: http://www.stillathomemom.com

Tanya is a friend of Rebecca's who has been a stay-at-home mom for a number of years, starting with the birth of her oldest child, Whitney, who is now grown and has kids of her own.

Rebecca asked her to contribute to this book because she knows Tanya personally and recognizes how well she manages her routines.

Here are her responses to the questions, along with her daily and weekly routines.

1. What challenges have you experienced when it comes to maintaining a daily routine for your particular situation?

As a stay-at-home mom of three kids in school, I am my own boss. This means I have no one holding me accountable for how I spend my time when I'm home alone. I know from experience that sticking to a daily routine helps me get things done, but no one is here to oversee me.

Back in the days when I worked in an office, I had deadlines to meet, bosses who were expecting things to be completed by a certain hour and co-workers surrounding me who could see firsthand how I spent my time. I couldn't get distracted in that setting because it would have been noticed. Being at home is different. While there is still plenty of work to get done, no one is around to motivate me to stay on task—except for me.

I tend to get distracted when I'm alone. I will see a jillion things that need to be done and my mind will jump from one thing to another. If I'm not careful, I can end up with 10 projects going at once and none of them getting done. A routine keeps me focused, helps me prioritize my work and assures my distraction-prone self that I will be getting everything done, in due time.

Lastly, the biggest challenge to maintaining a routine in my situation is this thing called life: It happens. A sick kid, orthodontist appointments (we have two kids in braces!), volunteer work, teacher conferences, lunch dates with friends, school assemblies, office parties and unforeseen errands—these are all examples of recent challenges I have faced in the past couple of weeks that disrupted my neatly planned routine!

2. How have you overcome these challenges?

Being aware of and admitting that I have challenges is the first step!

Some things that have helped me overcome my challenges are:

- Printing out a routine on paper. Having it all out there in front of me on a tangible piece of paper keeps me on task.
- Writing out a to-do list every night in bed (as part of my routine!).
- Setting a timer when I'm working on something so I can completely focus on it, without worrying about how long I've been doing it or when I need to move on.
- Including unplanned time blocks in my daily routine. This keeps me from being locked into a "schedule" and, thus, being inflexible.
- Keeping an ongoing "bucket list" of household projects I want to work on and allotting a time frame for that. These are things that are important to me but can wait because they're not urgent—such as organizing the garage or putting old photos in picture albums.

They are generally activities that may take months to complete but can be worked on in small increments of time. They may also be seasonal—such as addressing Christmas cards or wrapping gifts.

- Creating a personalized routine that works with my body's own unique circadian rhythms. While I have learned to love being an early bird (something that does not come naturally to me), no matter how hard I try, I cannot do focused work early in the morning.

I do less demanding work in the early mornings, such as checking emails, reading my favorite blogs and catching up on social media. I save writing, blogging and editing for mid-morning, when the house is quiet and my mind is at its sharpest.

I save exercise, cooking and housework for the afternoons, when I have pent-up physical energy and the household environment is becoming more active (with kids trickling in from school). I have a very busy mind at night when I'm settling down for bed, so I enjoy using that time for writing.

3. Give us a sample daily/weekly routine you use to you keep everything humming along.

MORNING ROUTINE

- Wake up, get showered and dressed for the day, put on makeup and fix hair. (This helps me wake up and puts me in a "take charge, this new day has begun" mode!)
- Quick wipe down of my bathroom, make bed (if husband is out of town; if he's not, then I make it later since he gets up later than me).
- Head downstairs; feed dogs and let them outside.
- If it is wintertime (November through April here!), it is an important part of my morning routine to turn on my Nature Bright therapy light. (I blogged about this here: http://bit.ly/1zDi1To)

- Make coffee; drink a big glass of water. Morning prayers to start my day and Bible or spiritual reading (10 to 15 minutes).

- Check email, read blogs, etc. (about one hour).

- I have an alarm set on my phone to tell me my "me time" is up. At this point, things get pretty busy. I unload the dishwasher, start a load of laundry, start making breakfast, make sure kids are getting up and around, do any early dinner/meal preparations that I can (for example, I may start something slow-roasting in the oven, start a loaf of bread in the bread machine or assemble a salad), set out lunches and add ice packs, clean up breakfast dishes and, finally, drive my kids to school.

- Back home from dropping off kids at school; switch laundry, do any quick cleanup (make bed if necessary), check kids' rooms and bathroom, etc. (I need a tidy environment to do my focused work).

- Writing and blogging—I am a new blogger and am finding I have to schedule time to blog regularly. It doesn't "just happen." Mid-mornings work best for me because my mind is sharp and the house is quiet. I take a lunch break if I notice I'm hungry, but I do not have one "scheduled." Sometimes I use this time to run errands, but generally this is my writing and blog work time.

- After writing and before the kids start coming home from school, I may spend some time working on a project from my ongoing "bucket list" that I referred to above. I don't have a set time for this, so I play it by ear according to my goals at the time. Sometimes I decide not to work on my bucket list and keep writing.

AFTERNOON ROUTINE

- Shortly before the kids start coming home from school, I put away my blogging and project work and spend some time completing daily and weekly household chores:

switching the laundry as needed, hanging/folding clothes, taking care of a weekly chore and running the vacuum in the main living area. I want them to come home to a neat, tidy environment to begin homework in.

- Prep/set out snacks for the kids to nibble on while doing homework.
- Once the kids get home, they get a snack, talk about their day and then begin homework. I use this time to do a little more housework (finish up laundry), run errands and exercise (go for a run and/or take the dogs for a walk). If I've exercised hard, I take a five-minute shower and freshen up my hair and makeup.
- Start dinner, set table and feed dogs; let dogs outside.
- Dinner with family at 6:00 (on most days).

EVENING ROUTINE

- Kids have cleanup duty after dinner; they alternate between specific kitchen jobs weekly (*see side note*). I use this time to pack lunches (a great time to do this is after dinner, since leftovers make great lunches!), sweep and Swiffer the kitchen floor and take out the garbage.
- Family time (or homework, if not done).
- Around 9:00, the kids start getting ready for bed. They are all teens now and don't really need my supervision, but I have "trained" them their entire lives to have bedtime routines, which they abide by naturally now. They get dressed for bed, set out the next day's clothes, set their backpacks by the door and even fill their water bottles and put them in the fridge.
- A bedtime routine is very important for me, too. At about the same time as the kids, I get ready for bed. I have a routine of getting a glass of wine or cup of hot tea, putting on my pajamas, brushing and flossing my teeth, washing my face and planning the next day.

I will look at my calendar/planner to remind myself of what is happening the next day and add to the next day's to-do list. I check the weather forecast so I can plan my outfit.

I also go around the house and spend 5 to 10 minutes doing a quick pick-up—fluffing the couch pillows, washing stray cups, straightening rugs, etc.—because I love to wake up to a tidy house in the morning! I lock up and turn off lights.

- I head to bed with my MacBook, my Kindle, a glass of water and a notepad and pen. This is such a predictable routine that when my dogs see me gathering those items, they start following me—they know it's bedtime! I set my alarm, charge my phone and get into bed.

- In bed, I write. It is one of my favorite things to do to wind down at night. In fact, that is exactly what I am doing right now. After about 30 minutes of writing, I turn off the lights and read my Kindle or watch an episode of Seinfeld with my husband. The notepad I take to bed is for writing down ideas or thoughts that come to my overactive mind while I am trying to settle down for the night. I also add to my to-do list because I will inevitably think of things I need to do as I'm lying in bed. It helps me to stop worrying; I can write it down and let it go.

Side note: My kids have rotating kitchen duty. Since I have three equally capable teens living under the same roof, I have divided up the kitchen chores. Each week, the chores change. Here is how we assign kitchen duty:

(1*) **Table:** Clear everything off the table; wipe and dry. Wipe off chairs. Move chairs from table and sweep underneath. If dishwasher is full at suppertime, it is the job of whoever has Table Duty to unload it.

(2*) **Food and counters:** Put away all leftover food in proper containers and place in fridge; clear and wipe all counters except the counter next to the sink (since this is where dirty dishes accumulate); place rinsed, dirty dishes into sink or onto counter by sink.

(3*) **Dishwasher**. Load dishwasher. Any "leftover" dishes get rinsed and placed in the sink. Clean sink and surrounding counter.

My job is to wash any leftover dishes (if there are any) by hand.

WEEKLY ROUTINE

If I didn't designate certain days to do certain chores, they may never get done! These are things I do during my afternoon chore times, *in addition to* daily chores. I don't like having one "housecleaning day," so I break it up into smaller parts. Also, some days are designated for certain things in our family, which my kids love. For example, they know Mom and Dad always go out on Fridays and they know we do something together as a family on Saturdays.

- Mondays: Clean upstairs bathrooms; change towels.
- Tuesdays: Vacuum upstairs and stairwell.
- Wednesdays: Vacuum downstairs, empty all trash. Set garbage and recycling bins by curb.
- Thursdays: Dust furniture, sweep porch and patio, mop all hard floors.
- Fridays: Change bed sheets; clean downstairs bathroom; change towels. Date night with husband.
- Saturdays: Family time, cookout or eat out; family activity such as movie night, bowling, game night, etc.
- Sundays: Church and volunteer work with youth group.

4. In what way does your routine make your life better?

Having a routine makes life so much better for me. I can reach the end of each day knowing that I spent my time wisely and that I got the important things done. I don't go to bed worried about something that I forgot or that I didn't have time for.

Keeping a routine helps me live my life with purpose. I feel better knowing that those long projects I might never find time for otherwise (organizing that garage!) are a work in progress. When maintaining a routine, I always go to bed looking forward to the next day, which ensures a good, restful night's sleep. It is my philosophy that a better life begins with a good night's sleep—and what better way to accomplish that than by having a daily routine in place?

#2. Creative Artist

Name: Miss Kristin (Pedderson)

Role: Musician

Website(s):

http://bigfussrecords.com

http://misskristin.com

http://facebook.com/misskristin

http://facebook.com/bigfussrecords

There is a certain mystique surrounding super creative people (musicians, writers, artists, actors, etc.) We often think of them as tortured souls who have to suffer in order to create great art. In reality, the most successful artists understand the importance of routines and working on their craft on a daily basis.

In this profile, Miss Kristin talks about how daily routines have become a critical component of her musical career:

1. What challenges have you experienced when it comes to maintaining a daily routine for your particular situation?

My challenges have been to stay committed to taking breaks. Sometime it feels like I have so much to do that I often forget the importance of rest.

Also, because working towards my dream means working for myself and making all my own choices, I have to remember to choose a vacation now and again. That way I stay strong and refreshed to complete my goals.

2. How have you overcome these challenges?

By remembering the importance of enjoying the journey and not focusing 100 percent on the destination.

3. Give us a sample daily/weekly routine you use to keep everything humming along.

My days have been dedicated to the art and craft of songwriting and performance for over 20 years. The days and months have varied as I have developed, but I still stick with much of the same routine.

I start my day with coffee, meditation and writing. I use my mental energy in the morning for writing lyrics (my passion) and/or PR (writing and telling my story). This happens in the first few hours of the day, say between 9 and 11 a.m. Then I take a break and enjoy an aerobic workout to get my physical energy flowing. This is very important, for without regular exercise I could not imagine becoming a great performer.

After the aerobic segment, I enjoy my lunch break. I relax a bit after lunch until 1 p.m., when I begin my vocal practice. This is a time to sing my favorite songs and/or practice my set list. I usually sing for one hour, after which I head back to the gym to do strength training and weight lifting. This has always felt very necessary for me to have a strong physique and performance style.

When I am done with strength training, I head into the steam room at the gym and do 45 minutes of breath work. This is to open my breathing and keep my mucous membranes moist. At first I disliked the breath work, but, after some time, what was my prison became my sanctuary. Now I love it and cannot live without it.

Finally, in the evening, I work part-time, usually doing online marketing or hairdressing. When I am not working, I work on creating mixes and productions on my computer, instrumentation and other miscellaneous tasks related to releasing my music. I do this type of schedule Monday through Friday only. On Saturdays and Sundays, I allow myself to rest, work more at my "real job" (hairdressing) and take a break from the routine.

Today I have many releases and have come full circle. I believe discipline is the secret to success. There are ways I wish I was even more disciplined, and I always strive to continue to keep my focus as I mature.

I don't allow distractions. I tell my friends and family that I am working when they call. Music is my full-time job. I made a conscious choice to focus on my music career over having a family. I did not believe I could have both and do both well. One would suffer.

In the first 10 years, I wrote 2,000 songs and felt it was a calling. I had to choose either the language or the kiss. I chose the language. My friends understand my career hours because I keep them as work hours. Time off feels normal, with nights and weekends available for get-togethers.

4. In what way does your routine make your life better?

My routine provides a great sense of accomplishment as I see progress in completing my goals, especially physical gains. Everyone measures progress differently. Some measure it by money, some by physical strength and others by personal achievements.

My routine allows me to stay focused and see results via all of the above. I rest well at night knowing I stayed the course and followed my routine and plan.

#3. 9-to-5 Worker

Name: Dr. Luz Claudio

Role: Medical Research Scientist

Website: http://www.drluzclaudio.com

Most people have traditional 9-to-5 jobs, making it difficult to find balance among the six major areas of life. Fortunately, it is possible to get everything done if you're intentional with what you do every day.

One great example is Dr. Luz Claudio—a medical research scientist at a large medical center in New York City, and director of its Division of International Health. She's also the mother of a seven-year-old girl and wife to a successful musician who travels often.

Although she wasn't able to answer all four questions (probably because she's super busy), she did do a great job of describing how she manages all her daily responsibilities.

Give us a sample daily/weekly routine you use to keep everything humming along.

The key to my day is waking up before the rest of my family to work out and meditate. Without that time alone, I don't think the rest of my day would be as productive.

I don't usually have a set schedule because my workload varies so much from day to day. Instead, I implement a set of general guidelines for structuring my day. In the mornings, I do the things that require other people's input or the things I can prepare to delegate to someone else.

For example, if I am writing a scientific article for publication with another colleague, I generally do that first because then I can pass it on to the other person for their input. This is more efficient because then, while I am doing something else in the afternoon, that person may be working on the article. Similarly, if I have a project that I could prepare to delegate to an assistant, I do that in the morning so that the project can be running later that same day.

In the afternoons, I am usually doing work that only I can do, such as working on my grant proposals, developing new ideas, analyzing data, having meetings, etc. I do keep meetings to a minimum and always have a specific agenda or issue to discuss before I call for a meeting.

One of the tricks I use that has really increased my productivity is a game I play with myself called "Beat the Clock." When I have a project, such as writing a grant proposal, I first write an outline. Then I estimate how long it should take me to write each of the sections outlined. Once I've decided on that, I set a timer and go at it relentlessly with the intention of finishing the section before the alarm goes off. When I finish within the allotted time, I give myself a small reward such as a piece of chocolate or a break.

I used to have no set time for leaving the office. It was not unusual for me to leave the office at 11 p.m. Now, I live by this thought: "The work expands to fit the time allotted to complete it." If I decide that I MUST leave the office by 5 p.m., I know that I must complete my work by that time, and I rarely disappoint myself. Because of this, my productivity has increased a lot and I have time to be home with my daughter and husband.

I use my personal time to create my website and have another business. I also love salsa dancing and getting together with my friends.

#4. Entrepreneur—Small Business Owner

Name: Steve Scott

Role: Authorpreneur

Website: http://www.DevelopGoodHabits.com

There's a lot you can do every day as an entrepreneur. Because we make our own schedules, it's not always easy to stay disciplined. In a way, having a structured daily routine is the secret weapon to creating freedom and flexibility.

In this final profile, Steve (one of the authors) talks about how his daily schedule helps him stay focused on his business while giving him time to enjoy other activities.

1. What challenges have you experienced when it comes to maintaining a daily routine for your particular situation?

Identifying *what* to work on is a constant, daily struggle. As an entrepreneur, I'm faced with a seemingly infinite amount of opportunities. *What do I write next? Do I need to answer the 40 emails in my inbox? Should I pursue a new project that might take my business to the next level?* These are the questions I wake up to every morning.

The problem is, I don't have a boss telling me what's important. For many years, I began each day by working on the tasks that *seemed* urgent, but weren't critical to the success of my business—like checking email or social media.

Another related challenge is finding that elusive work-life balance. Often, I'd feel stressed and anxious because I wasn't "doing enough" in my business. This had a negative effect on my health and relationships.

2. How have you overcome these challenges?

I used a simple (but effective) productivity hack. I start each day by identifying two to four critical tasks and adding them to my Most Important Tasks (MITs) list. These are the tasks I work on first thing in the morning. The key here is to use specific metrics so I know whether I've accomplished my goals or not.

As an example, I'll create tasks like these:

- Write 2,000 words of the daily routine book.
- Record five podcast episodes for SelfPublishingQuestions.com.
- Complete conversations 1 / 2 / 3 / 4 (each number represents a specific meeting).
- Create a new squeeze page for the Develop Good Habits blog.

This small daily action has had a positive impact on my business *and* personal life. Each day, when I complete these tasks, I know the priority tasks have been accomplished. Even if something unexpected comes up in the afternoon, I know I've done the important tasks that drive my business forward.

3. Give us a sample daily/weekly routine you use to keep everything humming along.

MORNING ROUTINE

Usually, I'll wake up at around 7 a.m. and immediately start my habit-stacking routine, which includes the following tasks:

- Making my bed
- Washing my face
- Drinking a pint of lemon water
- Preparing and drinking a nutritious smoothie

- Reviewing my goals
- Writing down two to four important tasks for the day

I end this routine by completing a new habit I'm trying to build into my life. For example, I'm currently trying to master the 10-minute declutter habit.

Around 7:30 a.m., I head out for a walk. I always bring my iPhone to use the Stitcher app to listen to a variety of podcasts on topics such as self-publishing, Internet marketing and investing. Also, I keep the Evernote app in a key location on my phone—in case I want to record an idea from one of these podcasts

From 8 a.m. to 10 a.m., I do my first (and sometimes only) block of writing. Usually, I work on a Kindle book, blog post or piece of content. On occasion, I'll write something for my own personal enjoyment.

From 10 a.m. to 11 a.m., I'll do a few different things: work on a project, reply to messages from key members of my team or complete a number of small tasks. These activities typically relate to items on my MITs list. The benefit here is that they provide a break from writing, but they also help me improve my business.

AFTERNOON ROUTINE

From 11 a.m. to noon, I'll relax a little by eating lunch, reading a nonfiction book for 30 minutes, running a few errands or driving to a nearby Starbucks coffeehouse to get out of the house.

The 12:30 p.m. to 6 p.m. timeslot is very flexible. Depending on the day (and specific deadlines), I do a number of things: write for a few more hours, clear out my email inbox, work through the steps of a current project, record a few podcast episodes or outline a future idea.

EVENING ROUTINE

Six p.m. to 7:30 p.m. (or sometimes 8:30) is exercise time. I either do another walk (usually with my fiancée) or go for a run. If I'm training for a marathon, sometimes the long run will extend into the evening.

After 8 p.m. is relaxation time. My fiancée and I will eat dinner, do a little cleaning and basically unwind for the rest of the night.

At 11 p.m., I'll go to bed and do a little bit of fiction reading. I usually fall asleep around 11:30 p.m.

SPECIAL CONSIDERATIONS

The above was a "normal" day, but there are few weekly events that impact how my workday is structured.

I like to time-block my week so all conversations (podcast interviews, masterminds, collaborative sessions and networking) happen on Wednesdays. I typically have anywhere from two to six conversations on this day. As an introvert, having regular conversations requires a lot of energy, so I prefer to get them all done in a single day.

Every other Thursday, I drive down to my parents', which is an hour and a half from my home. Once there, my entire family goes to dinner. Then I spend the night at their place and we see a movie together the next the afternoon.

Finally, my Fridays are very flexible. Sometimes I'll work the whole day, but on other days I'll do a few things in the morning, then relax for the rest of the day and most of the weekend.

4. In what way does your routine make your life better?

It's helped me find that work/life balance that eludes many entrepreneurs. Sure, I don't work as many hours as some people do. (I typically put in 30 to 40 hours per week.) However, this is *very* focused work. With my MITs, actionable project lists and using the Pomodoro technique, I'm able to focus on critical tasks and ignore everything else.

The upshot of this focused schedule is that I have plenty of time to exercise, enjoy a few hobbies and spend time with the people I love. I feel that I live a well-rounded life because I've taught myself how to juggle all these random activities.

Of course, all of this will change when I have children. ☺

SECTION 10:

CONCLUSION

Three Final Thoughts...

We've reached the end of the book. No doubt you've discovered a number of ideas and strategies you can add to your daily life. Perhaps you were inspired by the sample routines provided by people just like you, or maybe you realized that it's not that hard to make small, positive adjustments to your life. Suffice it to say, we covered a lot of ground in this book. As we close things out, we'd like to remind you of three things:

#1. Beware of monkey mind.

We've talked about monkey mind—the tendency to allow distractions and stress to keep you from focusing on the important things—a few times in this book, and for good reason. The moment you add new habits or routines to your life, monkey mind will be sure to rear its ugly head.

Here's a reminder of two simple things you can do to beat it into submission:

- Let go of the mentality that you have to be great at everything.
- Recognize that you can't do it all and that you need to instead focus on the most important things.

Nobody is perfect. Ignore what other people (and society) tell you is important. You're not a bad person if you can't do it all. What it means is that you're human like the rest of us.

Simply identify what's important to you and your family, do your best at getting results in these areas and then happily ignore everything else.

#2. Manage your stress.

Stress is a big part of monkey mind. It's natural to experience fear, panic and anxiety. Something as small as an angry email—or even a sideways glance—from a boss, co-worker or friend can get you riled up. That is…if you *allow* these thing to get to you.

A better solution is to learn how to keep calm in tense situations the same way that police, firefighters and members of the military do.

Learn to practice what the Greeks call apatheia, which means "without passion or suffering."

You may notice that apatheia sounds very similar to the word "apathy," but an important distinction needs to be made: Apathy has negative connotations, but apatheia is a positive trait. It doesn't mean to be indifferent, but rather to take control of your emotions so that you can respond to whatever happens in a controlled manner.

We're not talking about a lack of emotions, but rather being able to control your emotions when things beyond your control occur. Getting angry, upset and frightened does nothing to fix the problems and instead makes it almost impossible to see potential solutions.

You may not be able to completely block your emotions when bad things happen. After all, you are only human—but you do have control over your response. So go ahead and give yourself permission to rage, cry or be scared—then take a deep breath and calmly deal with the situation.

If you defeat emotions with logic and *then* address your problems, you will be surprised at how much smaller and more manageable those problems become.

#3. Throw away your laundry list of obligations.

It's not necessary to fill your day with a laundry list of obligations. Instead, do your best to focus on the most important things and learn to let go of the things that just don't matter.

Richard Branson said, *"To me, business isn't about wearing suits or pleasing stockholders. It's about being true to yourself, your ideas and focusing on the essentials."*

Whether you're a businessperson, factory worker, stay-at-home mom or something else, the purpose of this book is to help you to be true to yourself and your ideas—regardless of the label that you have given yourself or had slapped on you by someone else.

Our hope is that, by following the principles in this book, you'll be empowered to focus on the essentials and become the best YOU can be, one tiny habit and one routine at a time.

We wish you the best of luck!

Steve "S.J." Scott

http://www.DevelopGoodHabits.com

Rebecca Livermore

http://www.ProfessionalContentCreation.com

Would You Like to Know More

You can learn a lot more about habit development in my other Kindle books. The best part? I frequently run special promotions where I offer free or discounted books (usually $0.99) on Amazon.

One way to get <u>instant notifications</u> for these deals is to subscribe to my email list. By joining not only will you receive updates on the latest offer, you'll also get a free copy of his book "77 Good Habits to Live a Better Life."

Check out the below link to learn more.

http://www.developgoodhabits.com/free-updates

Did You Like *Level Up Your Day?*

Before you go, we'd like to say "thank you" for purchasing our book.

You could have picked from dozens of books on habit development, but you took a chance to check out this one.

So a big thanks for downloading this book and reading all the way to the end.

Now we'd like ask for a *small* favor. **Could you please take a minute or two and leave a review for this book on Amazon.**

This feedback will help us continue to write the kind of books that help you get results. And if you loved it, then please let me know :-)

More Books by Rebecca

The Daily Entrepreneur: 33 Success Habits for Small Business Owners, Freelancers and Aspiring 9-to-5 Escape Artists

Blogger's Quick Guide to Writing Rituals and Routines

Content Repurposing Made Easy: How to Create More Content in Less Time to Expand Your Reach

More Books by Steve

The Daily Entrepreneur: 33 Success Habits for Small Business Owners, Freelancers and Aspiring 9-to-5 Escape Artists

Master Evernote: The Unofficial Guide to Organizing Your Life with Evernote (Plus 75 Ideas for Getting Started)

Habit Stacking: 97 Small Life Changes That Take Five Minutes or Less

To-Do List Makeover: A Simple Guide to Getting the Important Things Done

23 Anti-Procrastination Habits: How to Stop Being Lazy and Get Results in Your Life

S.M.A.R.T. Goals Made Simple: 10 Steps to Master Your Personal and Career Goals

115 Productivity Apps to Maximize Your Time: Apps for iPhone, iPad, Android, Kindle Fire and PC/iOS Desktop Computers

Writing Habit Mastery: How to Write 2,000 Words a Day and Forever Cure Writer's Block

Declutter Your Inbox: 9 Proven Steps to Eliminate Email Overload

Wake Up Successful: How to Increase Your Energy and Achieve Any Goal with a Morning Routine

10,000 Steps Blueprint: The Daily Walking Habit for Healthy Weight Loss and Lifelong Fitness

70 Healthy Habits: How to Eat Better, Feel Great, Get More Energy and Live a Healthy Lifestyle

Resolutions That Stick☐How 12 Habits Can Transform Your☐ew Year

All books can be found at http://www.developgoodhabits.com